Touched by God

In memoriam Dom Alan Rees OSB

1941–2005

Touched by God

Ten Monastic Journeys

Edited by
LAURENTIA JOHNS, OSB

Foreword by
HENRY WANSBROUGH, OSB

burns & oates

Published by Burns & Oates, a Continuum imprint

The Tower Building,	80 Maiden Lane,
11 York Road,	Suite 704,
London	New York
SE1 7NX	NY 10038

www.continuumbooks.com

First published 2008

British Library Cataloguing in Publication Data
A catalogue record for this book is available from the British Library.

ISBN 978–08601–2451–1 (paperback)

Typeset by BookEns Ltd, Royston, Herts.
Printed and bound in Great Britain by The Cromwell Press, Trowbridge, Wiltshire.

Contents

Contents

Acknowledgements

Thanks are due to the following for kind permission to quote from copyright sources:

To Faber and Faber: a line from 'The Man with the Blue Guitar' from *The Collected Poems of Wallace Stevens* (pub. 1954).

To Continuum International Publishing Group: an extract from *A Heart that Trusts, Journal 1979–81* by Brother Roger of Taizé (pub. 1986).

To Dom Ralph Wright OSB: the poem 'Waiting' from *Silence is their Music* (pub. Knots Press, 1979).

Foreword

One Friday evening when I was 17 I was picking a rugby team for the morrow, with the Ampleforth school captain and the coach. We had not finished our selection when the bell went for house evening-prayers. So the coach – whose name was Basil Hume – invited us to Compline. As we boys sat in the dark nave of the church, looking up at the lighted choir, I was deeply struck by the monastic combination of prayer and family, especially when the abbot went round saying 'Good-night' to each of his community by a sprinkling of holy water. Different aspects of the *Rule for Monks*, attributed to the shadowy figure of Benedict, appeal to different people. Basically, it codifies ways of living the Gospel values in community, but the variety of biographical sketches included in this volume – a successor to *A Touch of God*, penned by a new generation of nuns and monks – shows the variety of ways in which the *Rule* can be lived, even within one interpretation of the tradition.

Recently I was asked whether the Benedictines are a strict order: a puzzling question, quite apart from the mistaken idea that Benedictines constitute an 'order' in the modern sense of the word. Every house has its own spirit and individuality. Certainly, I did not feel that I could reply that we were a lax order. The *Rule*, as I hope these examples of ways of living it will show, seeks not to restrict but rather to inspire, to broaden rather than to narrow. A school sets out to discover and release the potential of its students, as does also this 'School of the Lord's service', so that the author of the *Rule* apologizes for prescribing anything 'harsh or burdensome' (Prologue) to prevent monks – as one great abbot put it – 'filing down the *aspera* and putting cushions on the *dura*' which constitute the road to God. The *Rule* won its place, its gradual adoption by monks and nuns all over Europe, in the later centuries of the first millennium, by its gentle, often self-deprecatingly humorous way of showing how Christ is to be seen as present in the community and in every person, but especially in those in need, by its sage and simple advice on prayer as the backbone of every Christian life, by its emphasis on the joy of loving service and of family endeavour.

It is hoped that the stories of individual nuns and monks presented here will demonstrate the diversity of ways in which the *Rule* has shaped some Christian lives. At any rate, on that Friday evening 55 years ago I never thought that my monastic apostolate would set me one week working for the Pontifical Bible Commission and the next penning these lines in the African bush, to the occasional background of the ominous roar of lions and the manic shriek of hyenas.

Henry Wansbrough, OSB
Laikipia Wilderness Education Centre,
Kenya/Ampleforth Abbey

Introduction

In 1982 the English Benedictine Congregation (EBC) brought out *A Touch of God*, a book in which monks and nuns shared something of their personal faith journeys and which has since seemed to speak to seekers beyond the cloister. Twenty-five years on, the appeal of monastic values such as silence, prayer and community appears undimmed, to judge from the response to the BBC television series *The Monastery*, filmed at Worth Abbey. And so we have been persuaded, mostly by an enthusiastic group of young people with an interest in things Benedictine, to bring out another set of journeys.

We make no apologies for following the same simple format as that of the original volume, the classic first-person narrative where the monk or nun, far from being a remote or ethereal figure, emerges as Everyman on a journey – essentially an interior one, in search of both 'the Other' and the true self. When Jacob wrestled with that mysterious figure – God? – at the Jabbok (Gen. 32.22ff.) and asked the name of his assailant, he was given instead his own new name, Israel, and with it, a blessing. In all ages the journey to God advances through growth in self-knowledge, a theme which runs through each journey presented here. Whereas individualistic self-seeking isolates, the authentic search for

1

self-knowledge leads to the blessings of communion and peace. 'Have peace in yourself', said St Seraphim of Sarov, 'and thousands around you will be saved'. To be engaged in that inner search for peace, is therefore, to be a peace-maker in our troubled world.

The world has not stood still, however, over the past quarter-century and this book differs from its predecessor in several ways. The decline in numbers of monks and nuns in most of our monasteries has led, happily, to an increased sense of interdependence, both within the Congregation and between Congregations, and has been more than balanced by the phenomenal growth of interest in the Benedictine life outside its permanent vowed expression. In recognition of these shifts, we are delighted to welcome as guest contributors Joanna Gilbert, a young member of the Lay Community of St Benedict (founded in 2003, see www.laybenedictines.org), and Dom Andrew Nugent, a veteran monk of Glenstal Abbey in the Congregation of the Annunciation. Advances in technology since the 1980s have also made it feasible to include contributions from some of the English Benedictine monasteries in the United States, and while, regrettably, it has not been possible to represent all 13 of the EBC houses, these may be visited at www.benedictines.org.uk. While very much a corporate venture, this work remains the expression of the individual contributors.

I am most grateful to all who have helped to foster this book with practical advice, encouraging words, positive criticism and prayer. Abbot President Richard Yeo has been unfailingly supportive, as have members of the EBC Monastic Theology Commission; Dame Maria Boulding, Editor of the original *A Touch of God*, has been most generous and sensitive in sharing her experience; Dom Francis Straw (Buckfast) has always been on hand to advise on technicalities, while Abbot Geoffrey Scott of Douai has more than once given a timely 'word'. We are indebted to Linda Jones for her insightful comments in the early stages of the project, to Shirley Scott for both moral and professional support, and to all at Continuum for their expertise and kindly assistance throughout.

Last but not least, I should like to thank my co-contributors for their patience, succour and friendship. Our world, at least in the West, is short on hope. In his conclusion Dom Andrew Nugent has, I think, put his finger on what we have been trying to do: *to give an account of the hope that is in all of us* (cf. 1 Pet. 3.15). These journeys are offered in the hope that they might, in some small way, help to light the way for others. That way is Jesus Christ.

Laurentia Johns OSB
Stanbrook Abbey, Pentecost 2007

1

'One Step Enough For Me'

Joanna Gilbert

My journey has barely begun. Life is largely a blank canvas, but with some significant hints and intuitions beginning to sketch out the scene. At 26, I'm not in religious vows and have not yet made a definitive choice of life path. So in what sense is mine a monastic journey?

I would say I'm in a process of discernment, grappling with the question of whether the Benedictine vows of obedience, stability and *conversatio morum* (a promise to be faithful to the monastic way of life) will form the fundamental structure in which I live my life. Certainly, I've been formed by monastic influences, leading me to a place where – though not in a traditional cloister – my daily living is guided by St Benedict's Gospel vision. For nearly two years I've been resident in a small, urban community of young lay people committed to a rhythm of prayer and work in common, inspired by Benedict's *Rule*. But the life here has so far involved only a temporary commitment, and so the next step is looming.

Vocation is deeply mysterious. To discover and embrace God's call is to take a step each day into the unknown, carving out the path to God that is uniquely mine. The invitation has been to patience and trust, struggling to reach a point where I can say 'one step enough for me'[1] – not in

4

control of the future, nor with inside knowledge as to where God may be leading, but simply open and listening, trying to say with as much of me as will consent at any time, 'Here I am Lord. I'm coming to obey your will.'

I've found reflecting on the patterns of my personal history has meant tuning in to a deeper intuition of knowing who I am and beginning to hear the name by which I'm called. It's a journey of becoming more human and discovering my true self. But ours is always a limited view. Though the future is full of uncertainty, I can say something about the landscape of the journey so far, identifying a few themes that seem to recur.

'BEFORE I FORMED YOU IN THE WOMB ...' (JER. 1.5)

To tell this story properly I must begin about ten years before my birth. In 1971, my father went to university. Previously he'd been educated for five years by the Benedictines at Worth School in Sussex, and during his first year at Oxford he became friends with a fellow student who had also been educated by Benedictines, though at Downside. Peter Jamison – later to be Abbot Christopher of Worth – approached my father sometime in 1972 asking if he was aware of the new developments happening at Worth Abbey involving students staying alongside the monastic community. And so that summer my father returned for a week to his former boarding school, with his university friend, to live and pray alongside the monks, while running a holiday for inner-city boys.

At this time, what was later to become known as the Worth Abbey Lay Community was in its initial stages. The beginnings seem to stem from the Easter of 1971 when a group of students from Southampton University attended the monastery's celebration of Easter. Previously, Easters were mainly attended by Worth School 'old boys', but that year a letter had been sent out from the community to numerous chaplaincies, inviting students to attend.

After Easter the students from Southampton asked Abbot Victor Farwell whether he was open to the idea of allowing young lay people to stay for longer and experience more of the monastic way of life. He was interested in giving the experiment a go. In the course of 1972 a residential lay community took shape at Worth. It would appear that Abbot Victor, not averse to taking risks, saw the need to make monastic life visible beyond the traditional recruitment ground of Benedictine education, which had been the key source of vocations in the past but whose effect was now dwindling. In the second full year of residency, after graduating from Oxford, my father joined a group of eight other young people living in a series of former stables, renovated largely by unskilled student volunteers. Legend has it that my father built an entire wall that was later discovered to be structurally supported on one brick! Over subsequent years the Lay Community developed a greater outreach to chaplaincies, offering hospitality to groups every weekend, many summer service projects, and the large celebration of the Easter Liturgy.

Having recently graduated, my mother visited Worth to stay in the Lay Community in 1972, and came for her first Easter in 1973. On arrival in the front quad of the main school building on Maundy Thursday – in torrential rain – my father welcomed her out of the taxi and offered to carry her luggage. In September 1975 my parents were the first Lay Community couple to be married in the newly-built Abbey Church.

'THE FREEDOM OF THE CHILDREN OF GOD'
(ROM. 8.21)

Born in January 1981, I was the second child of three, all girls. My parents chose to settle in Sussex after they were married, presumably partly so they could be near Worth. So until the age of 11 I grew up in a small town called Haywards Heath, five miles from the Abbey, and the most striking feature of my childhood was the unusual experience of growing up in close relationship with a monastery and as part of a vibrant group of young Christians. Until I was about 5, we 'commuted' to Sunday Mass at Worth, and each year would attend a large gathering of Lay Community members over the August bank holiday as well as the Easter celebrations. At weekends it was quite usual to be up at Worth having picnics or going for walks in the woods with other families living nearby. The strongest memories I have from these first few years of my life are of careering around the estate with my sisters and other children, many of whose parents had similarly met and married through the Lay Community. While Abbot Victor's experiment proved a great success for vocations into the novitiate during the 1970s, there were also many marriages. Over the years the children became a solid tribe of all ages, and one of the greatest gifts of my life has been the ongoing friendships made from birth.

Worth seemed a magical place to a child. When the boys from the school were away during holidays we would have access to the various buildings, old and new, across the campus and would roam around exploring every nook and cranny. There was a great sense of freedom for us as children at Worth. The community had an atmosphere of 1970s spontaneity: at times chaotic, but full of life, no doubt characteristic of a group made up of so many students and young families at a time in the Church – so soon after

7

Vatican II – when the new life of the Resurrection seemed very close.

As far as I can recollect, I didn't have any great sense of God's presence as a child. Nor did I have any simple certainty of his existence. This profound experience of Christian community, however, seemed to connect with the very heart of the Gospel message for me. I knew in it a great sense of Easter joy and Christian freedom. It formed a deep-rooted image of God, and of what it meant to live the Christian life. I felt a sense of belonging at Worth, of being at home, and of being in a place where I could most fully be myself. My awareness of this grew considerably in my late teens, and played its part in a fairly radical change of life direction in my early twenties. Both my parents were social workers and the Lay Community was full of people in caring professions which also incarnated for me the teachings of Jesus. Though I don't think I particularly recognized Jesus as divine, I sensed in him the answer to life. At some level I knew the Christian call was to follow the pattern of his life: to journey through the Cross.

As a child I also had little awareness of the life of the monks at Worth; this was simply part of the backdrop of my childhood: something that did not influence me in any explicit sense, but more by osmosis. The monks themselves, however, were important figures to me and a source of great fascination. A certain quality about them meant I felt comfortable in their presence. When I was probably no more than 3 years old, one particular novice had to put up with me bringing a comb to Mass each week so that I could comb his hair! There was a quality about the monks I knew then, and have since discovered to be common to men and women living the Benedictine way, that attracts me at a very deep level, and makes me long to be in some sense part of this family of people.

8

We found, living so near Worth, that monks' visits were a regular feature of our family life. My parents' choice of Fr Dominic Gaisford as my godfather was a great blessing to me, and though he was often away at Worth's foundation in Peru, when back in England, he would usually make a visit. Tired and in need of some care and relaxation, he would come for a meal and always need a nap on the sofa before driving home. I think the humanity of the monks had a deep impact on me. As I've become familiar with the themes of Benedictine life in recent years, I've perhaps been most struck by the sense in which Benedict's framework for Christian living creates the conditions for nurturing people to become more fully themselves. In his 'school of the Lord's service', as Benedict calls the monastery in the Prologue to his *Rule*, we flourish by learning to inhabit ourselves. Thomas Merton, the American Trappist, talks of the call to become the 'particular poet' or 'particular monk' we have been created to be, not striving to be someone else or leaping hurdles in trying to live up to a false image of self. The anxious perfectionist in me makes this a constant temptation. I think the monastic way offers a much simpler invitation: to surrender, to let go of striving and become fully human in our uniqueness. Dominic was 'himself': very much at ease with his humanity, a warm and tactile person who attracted others to him. As a child I would always feel a desire to be near him. One particular afternoon when he had eaten lunch with us and was fast asleep on the sofa, I sat with my older sister at his feet watching him, his head tilted back and mouth open. Devising a plot, we got some sugar crystals from the kitchen and popped them in his mouth to see what he would do. We waited for him – totally undisturbed in his nap – to wake up. Gradually, he gently ground his teeth, and a crunching noise began. A small frown came across his brow, at which point, a little bemused

9

and dazed, he woke up, looked at us and our mischievous grins, and smiled in knowing solidarity with our cheeky act of affection.

'DARKNESS IS NOT DARK FOR YOU'
(PS. 138[139].12)[2]

When I was 11 my father applied for a senior management position in Staffordshire Social Services and one evening brought home the news that he had got the job. For me, this induced a terrible sinking feeling mixed with great exhilaration at something so new. I'd never really known any significant experience of change in my life, so I viewed the move more with curious excitement than with fear. Despite this, I would now term the reality of the experience as 'root shock'. I wasn't at all prepared for the confusion I would feel. On 8 June 1992 we moved from our safe and familiar town in a county where the landscape – green and picturesque – was known and loved, to Stafford in the Midlands, situated between the industrial city of Stoke-on-Trent, and the former mining communities of the Black Country. Stafford struck me as bleak, and the people seemed entirely alien. During the first few months I developed regular stomach aches, and would avoid going to school as much as possible. For years I found it tremendously hard to make friends. I felt no connection with anyone: my sense of familiarity was entirely removed. I felt disconnected with my environment and with myself and all the security I had known up until this point. The next few years were turbulent for everyone in my family. Both my sisters reacted in a similar way to the move. Mary was 13 and well into teenage rebellion, and I was just entering that inevitably painful time of change and insecurity: the shift from childhood into the in-between time of adolescence. No doubt a little prematurely, the move marked the end of my childhood.

About a year after arriving in the Midlands, aged only 12, I entered a period of my life that I recognized to be dark: a phase of rebellion where I was testing out the boundaries. Always one for leading the way, I began inspiring my friends to smoke cigarettes and truant from school, and, by Christmas of that year, was leading a large wave of anti-social behaviour within my year group. Much of what I did during that phase was fairly trivial, but I was very young and could feel the weight of it on my conscience. Soon I was longing for the recovery of innocence and wholesomeness again. It has always been in my personality to have a strong moral conscience, but also to be wilful and prone to black moods and outbursts. Ever since, there has been a battle within to integrate this seemingly conflicting rebellious streak with the side of me that hungers and thirsts for righteousness.

At that time I had the first of what was to become a recurring experience which I would later recognize as grace trying to break through into my life. I felt a sense of the sacred by virtue of distance and the comparison of light with dark. Shortly before Christmas, 1993, I got myself into a web of lies over an incident at school, and felt so deeply disconcerted at the darkness of it all and my own ability to deceive myself that I made a decision to turn over a new leaf.

During my teenage years I began making independent visits to Worth, heading off on the train and travelling across London by Tube. Worth began to provide activities for the growing number of Lay Community children now hitting their teens. Three times a year, weekends were laid on by adult volunteers, and friends from all corners of the country would make their way to the Abbey. The group

11

developed its own identity and a strength of friendship that was of an entirely different nature from the friendships we held with peers in the socially pressured environment of school. As teenagers at Worth, we found a culture of acceptance, a freedom to be ourselves and a sense of belonging which we all craved. Adolescence is often characterized by a great sense of loneliness and a yearning for intimacy and connection. We cultivated this at Worth, and the friendships were enduring.

My experience of Worth altered quite considerably after our move. When we lived close by we didn't often stay at Worth but would commute for Lay Community events by day. Now that we were 180 miles away, Easter, in particular, took on a new importance in my life. Over the next 15 years I stayed for the Easter Triduum, arriving on Maundy Thursday and departing after Easter Sunday morning Mass. Easter began to impact on the heart of my faith and on my understanding of myself at a level much deeper than my conscious awareness as I took in the drama of the liturgy each year. It anchored each year in a powerful experience of humanity's Redemption, a drama played out through each one's personal history.

Increasingly, though, life was split into two separate realities: Stafford and Worth, and generally the two did not cross over. It was the Easter when I was 15 that I had a second experience of grace trying to break in. I'd suffered mild depression for some years, but that weekend it was as if the fog cleared and I felt life flowing in my veins. At the services my face would burn red and I had a sense of the sacred being close, though I didn't really attach the name 'God' to this experience. On leaving Worth, my depression was gone and didn't return.

12

'IS THERE ANYONE HERE WHO YEARNS FOR LIFE?' (*RB*, PROLOGUE, 15)

Despite turning over a new leaf at 12, by 14 I was back into smoking, drinking and testing the boundaries in different ways. But being a little older, it certainly didn't feel so sordid. Perhaps the motivation behind it all had changed. I'm able to look back now and see that essentially I was hungry for life: full of an aching desire for happiness, finding temporary fulfilment in peak experiences. But I don't think it had much to do with escapism or a revolt against goodness: more a yearning to grasp hold of life and to prolong the moment. The intensity of experience was high: we had tremendous fun.

This thirst for life, I've since discovered, Benedict refers to in his Prologue. The Lord, seeking workmen, calls out 'Is there anyone here who yearns for life?' The monastic is a seeker of 'true and eternal life' (*RB*, Prologue, 17). My discernment is to discover where I will find true life. The search for happiness will always mean confronting that paradox Christ presents in the Gospels: if we truly wish to find fulfilment we must lose our lives by offering life to others and building our life in God alone.

Shortly before my seventeenth birthday, at a fancy dress Christmas party wearing 70s clothes dug out from my parents' wardrobe and a large, bronze Taizé cross around my neck, I met Andy, with whom I began a relationship. After a few months we were meeting up almost every night. I moved into his world, adopting his friends and way of life. This new circle was made up of a rather eccentric mix of odd and zany characters. While I had a great affection for them, the worlds we'd grown up in were very different, their values at times at odds with my Catholic upbringing, and their view fairly parochial. Increasingly, mine and Andy's

13

outlooks jarred, and I began to feel I was being false in fitting myself into someone else's world. I didn't know then who I was myself, so I formed my identity in relation to him. This left me uneasy: I sensed I needed to be a more developed person before joining myself to someone else.

When in the sixth form, for a reason still unclear to me, I decided, along with a group of friends, to join the diocesan pilgrimage to Lourdes. None of us was explicitly interested in religion, but somehow – in God's Providence – a noble streak in us beckoned, a desire to serve others. In May 1998, just five months into my relationship with Andy, we set off for Lourdes, travelling overnight in couchettes. That week I was confronted by real doubt about Andy. As I'd always found at Worth, when in a faith context I felt more authentically myself and alive. I was faced with the question of whether Andy was really the kind of person I wanted to be with. He wasn't Christian, and expressed no interest in anything spiritual. I wondered if I shouldn't be with a nice Catholic boy, with whom I could share this dim sense of faith I had, that seemed – though as yet so unexplored – nonetheless to be at the core of me and my perspective on life. When I returned to England I spent two days sweating over the question of whether I should call it quits with Andy. I was standing at a crossroads.

We stayed together and within two months had begun sleeping together, a situation I drifted into rather than making any considered choice. I felt uninformed as to the reasons why the Church says we should wait until marriage. I lacked grounding in Catholic teaching and had no role models I could relate to. As we got to know each other better, a deep attachment to Andy grew. He became my best friend. Despite the lack of common ground, as two personalities we shared a great deal. Our relationship was very affectionate and playful, and I adored him.

Over the years I spent with Andy I seemed to become increasingly uncertain of my direction in life: I was drifting. After a failed first attempt at starting university, I began studying Fine Art at Leeds University a year later, feeling thoroughly indifferent to the subject. These feelings of dissatisfaction grew. I never went to the Chaplaincy in my first year, nor did I make any Christian friends. With hindsight, I can see the extent to which I was burying my spirituality: a deeply rooted morality was trying to work its way to the surface and was certainly playing a part in a growing feeling of uneasiness. At that time, my gang of Lay Community contemporaries had grown to adulthood, and while the strong network of friendships and sense of belonging continued, organized events waned. Unformed in our faith and unlikely to find much support in parishes, most of us stopped going to church. It was during Easter at Worth in my first year at university that someone suggested we go to Taizé, the community in France we'd all heard of but knew little about. With a burst of motivation, I said I'd organize a trip. That summer a group of eight young people set off by coach to Burgundy.

This was my first real experience of a monastic community beyond Worth, and I was immediately impressed by the sense of clarity of the Gospel message. Br Roger, the founder and leader of the community, held a simple but profound vision of Christian living: his themes were trust, hope, and joy. Although much of what Taizé was about washed over me on my first visit, it sowed seeds that germinated over the course of that year. While at Taizé I felt a strong urge to get involved in running new and existing events for teenagers at Worth. So, on my return I joined the team of leaders at weekends and also started planning an activities week for teenagers for the following summer.

'YOUR HAND EVER LAID UPON ME'
(PS. 138[139].5)

At Easter 2002 I left Andy as usual on Maundy Thursday to travel down to Worth. Nothing in our relationship had noticeably changed. We never really argued and had certainly not fallen out of love: in fact, the relationship had the potential to go on and on, very possibly to marriage. Yet that Easter something unexpected began to happen. A change was set in motion that overwhelmed me: a series of experiences and coincidences that I knew to be 'supernatural'. Arriving at Worth, I found myself speaking to friends about love, relationships and marriage, expressing enthusiastic consent to the Church's teaching on sexual morality. The words seemed to be coming from somewhere other than me, yet I felt a deep conviction of the truth of what I was saying. My heart was burning within me as I spoke. On Good Friday I went to confession and spoke for the first time to a monk about my relationship with Andy, something which began to open the floodgates to grace and the possibility of making the decision to change my lifestyle.

That weekend we were led by Fr Mark Barrett, a monk of Worth, in reflections on the theme of 'Journey' and the 'landscape of our lives'. His images and analogies resonated with me. I had the image of standing upon a shore, afraid to enter into life by diving into the sea. It became more apparent than ever that life had more to offer than the thin existence I was living. In groups we were invited to do *lectio divina* or spiritual reading on Psalm 138[139]. My God – if indeed I believed in a God – was distant from me, but in this Psalm I began to recognize his closeness. The words I was drawn to over and over were 'your hand ever laid upon me'. For the first time that weekend I also recognized that the person I was at Worth was the person I really wanted to be:

I think I started then to realize that I didn't need to be split between two worlds, but could allow the Gospel into my everyday life and become a more authentic person as a result. I was discovering my true self.

On Easter Monday, to buy more time to think through what was happening, I went with friends to the 'Celebrate' Conference in North Devon, a week-long Catholic charismatic event with 1500 people. On the first morning of talks for young adults the coincidence was too much: the theme was 'Love, sex and relationships'! I sat through various talks where people told their personal stories, and it was as if every word were addressed directly from God to the core of me. The talks presented God's loving vision for human sexuality: quite the opposite of my life-denying impression of the Church's teaching. Three-quarters of the way through the input, I'd heard all I needed. Turning to a friend, I left the hall, and outside broke down in a flood of tears knowing I'd made my decision: I would have to leave Andy.

The God I encountered that week was the God of truth, whose truth is inescapably compelling in its promise of freedom. At 'Celebrate' I was prayed over by a couple who laid on hands like the early Christians, and I experienced an otherworldly peace welling up from deep within and overwhelming me, liberating me to allow God free movement in my life. I discovered God's love is above all mercy. I was one of the strays whom he seeks out; I could feel something inside calling me home. I don't now regret having strayed because of the great gift of experiencing the joy of forgiveness. St Augustine's words speak to me:

I have drifted to the things of below and have become darkness. But from there – even from there I have deeply loved you. I have wandered and have remembered you. I heard your voice telling me to

17

come back but I did not hear properly in the tumult of arguments. And now here I am returning to you, burning and panting towards your source. Let no one take me from it.[3]

'IN PATHS THAT THEY HAVE NOT KNOWN I WILL GUIDE THEM' (ISA. 42.16)

My Easter encounter with the living God became the pivotal point of my life to date. Shortly after, I began a year of study at the University of California. Over the course of that year I started reading spiritual books, especially by monastic authors, and discovered a yearning for prayer. God often felt tangibly close. It was on returning to England that I first sensed an attraction to religious life. I'd always assumed I'd marry, but suddenly the thought dawned on me that I might be called to celibacy. Initially, the attraction wasn't specifically to monastic life. I was largely motivated by a burning sense of the importance of serving others, and in particular a desire to work with the poor. Celibacy seemed to offer a radical freedom to love: throwing everything away in order to do what was right and true. With St Paul I wanted to say 'I count everything as loss' (Phil. 3.8) for the advantage of knowing Jesus. I couldn't then understand how marriage and children could be compatible with living out the Gospel in a wholehearted way, an attitude I am now beginning to see is horribly misguided.

I spent three weeks at Taizé that summer, including one in silence, which gave me space to ponder this question further. I think at first I imagined the answer would come straight away: that it would simply drop out of the sky. Later I could appreciate vocation as entering in trust into a mystery that gradually unfolds as God's revelation of love:

that I am made by Love, and that Love is the name by which he calls me to return to him. In that week of silence my heart was opened to the creative truth of monastic values. Benedict's theme of listening opened me to begin hearing and seeing God incarnate in all of his Creation. Around that time I remember reading about the People of Israel's concept of how God speaks to us: that we are in existence solely because God is communicating with us in every moment, speaking us into being, and that if he ceased to speak, we would cease to exist. As the practice of praying with Scripture grew, I became increasingly tuned in to hear this voice of God breathing life into me through Scripture, but also through every other aspect of life. And in this encounter moment to moment with Love, I felt that process of moulding and shaping begin: the gentle transformation that is brought about when we stand vulnerable before God. In prayer, we dare to show God who we are: to reveal our face as he shows his to us. I lost my fear of silence in Taizé. Silence was not empty, but full of the joy of God.

At about this time the Lay Community was set a historic challenge by the new Abbot of Worth, Fr Christopher Jamison. We were invited to 'leave home', as it were, and to become an independent lay Benedictine community or movement, in the style of the new movements thriving in parts of Europe. The lay and monastic communities had very different needs, and both had evolved considerably over 30 years. The flow of residents had dried up, Lay Community membership was now spread all across the country and abroad, and so the focus on Worth, situated in the south-east, was not always helpful or practical. It was indeed time for a change in direction. We needed a renewal and to discover a vision for lay living taking inspiration from the *Rule of St Benedict* in a way appropriate to our varied lives. The Lay Community responded well to the challenge which brought to a close – with sadness and expectant joy – our community's life as a dependent offshoot of Worth.

I felt great enthusiasm to be part of the newly named Lay Community of St Benedict, and wanted to find ways to outreach with Benedict's vision for Christian living. Returning to Leeds for the final year of my degree, I began organizing a programme of retreats at Manchester and Leeds University Chaplaincies, as well as weekend retreats at Worth, focused on prayer and community-building, with formation on Benedictine themes. Fr Rod Jones, a monk of Worth, was given permission by the Abbot, keen to support new initiatives which reached out to others in the Church and beyond, to act as chaplain to these events, giving talks on themes like obedience, stability, conversion of life, and how to create sanctuary in our lives. Delving into the *Rule* gave my search roots, taking me to the heart of the Gospel while providing a practical and concrete guide for trying to centre my life on the person of Christ.

My final year in Leeds was full of activity and demanding work levels: the course was time-consuming and, on top of that, I was heavily involved in the Catholic Chaplaincy and was elected to serve on the Council of the Lay Community of St Benedict. I could have been in danger of getting things very out of balance, except that, increasingly, I felt this deep yearning for prayer: a call to the lonely place. When running a weekend at Worth I would arrive a day or two early and stay on afterwards to give room to this desire for solitude. I spent ever-increasing amounts of time at Worth, finding that the capacity for prayer expanded; a space in me was being carved out for God. Giving that time to reflection opened my eyes to recognize the sacramental quality of all Creation. I became tuned in to the changing seasons, the cycles and rhythms of nature as I saw the landscape at Worth with a contemplative gaze, passing through the death of winter and into the new life of spring. Watching the same view shifting with the different light and seasons – in autumn caught in the strong declining sun, illuminated gold and singing God's glory – I found the landscape would resonate in me. I felt drawn by a single-hearted desire to be still and see God here and now, in touch with the sacred in the present moment.

'WHY CAN I NOT FOLLOW YOU NOW?'
(JN 13.37 NJB)

The theme of unknowing has pervaded my experience of God, both in prayer and in external circumstances. Every step we take with God is a call into darkness, a stepping out of the boat with St Peter to walk on water. Our desire to be near Christ is the motivating force which gives us the reckless trust we need to risk everything, letting go of all that brings us security in order to rely on him alone. My last year at Leeds was like stepping out of the boat. I was called to follow a dull intuition, and knew God's tremendous Providence when we place everything in his hands. The things I felt called to do didn't even seem to exist, so I had to hand myself over in trust to see if I was being invited to carve out a new path. Talking with friends, monks of Worth and the Council of my Community, a vision slowly took shape for establishing a new residential Benedictine community experience for young adults. On finishing at Leeds, I committed myself to work for a year developing the proposal into a reality. Brighton became the focus of our attention: we found a house with a low rent in a lively city parish. Everything fitted into place. So, in August 2005, with three others from the Lay Community of St Benedict, we set out on an adventure in Benedictine living, praying the Office together three times a day, committed to personal prayer and *lectio divina*, working on common projects of service and evangelization, while pooling incomes from part-time jobs. So here I still am in my second year in Brighton as part of the Elm Grove Community (named after the road on which we live).

Prayer is at the heart of all we do here. It seems to me that once we've entered into that journey of prayer we find it transforms, bit by bit, every part of our reality. Prayer is not separate from anything else: we discover through it a unity between all things in our life; that we are held in him, who is the source of all life. The call is continually to trust, to let go of control and be empty-handed before God, holding on to nothing for ourselves but clinging to him alone. My natural tendency is to hold the reins of control very tightly and to want to know the way ahead. In prayer I hear the invitation to surrender, to leave the props behind, and to fall into the hands of the living God. St Peter offers me great encouragement. I identify with his zeal, and his failure to live up to his own strong desire to follow the Lord: 'Why can I not follow you now? I will lay down my life for you.' Jesus answered, 'Lay down your life for me? ...In all truth I tell you, before the cock crows you will have disowned me three times' (Jn 13.37-38 NJB). We try and we fail, and in our failure we are broken open to receive the free gift of the Resurrection.

Prayer is a journey layer by layer towards the truth of ourselves that starts with some thread of self-knowledge: something solid and real within. In making contact with the truth of ourselves we touch God because he is present in reality: there in the facts. For me prayer often begins in an inner place of woundedness or fear, or in the discovery of barricaded doors. At times I've hit with horror my own emptiness, the lack of love and the unwillingness to be selfless, the reality of how little I am truly willing to follow

Christ in self-surrender. Like St Peter I want to believe I am ready and willing wholly to renounce myself and take up my cross, but I fall into the trap of romanticism: placing great emphasis on some grand act of heroism somewhere in the future, while avoiding the true place of Gospel choice, the mundane here and now. Living in daily contact with God through Scripture, prayer and community brings at times an overwhelming awareness of how far we are from embodying our true humanity. So, on our knees, we turn again to Christ – knowing our need of a Saviour – to ask for his gift of transforming grace. This recognition of our weakness is the key to salvation. It is Benedict's central theme of humility: a profound invitation to see ourselves in a truthful light, as God sees us, with an honest but loving gaze. It is about becoming fully human by living earthed in the truth.

In prayer I return continually to the person of Jesus, attracted to his humanity as he beckons, saying, 'Come to me all who labour and are heavy laden and I will give you rest ... Learn from me, for I am gentle and lowly in heart' (Mt. 11.28-29). It is here in the gentle humanity of the Word made flesh that I discover a resonance with my truest self: a person without armour, freed from fear and falsehood. Monastic values should gradually free a person to become 'real', liberated from our attraction to illusion. In Plato's allegory, we are prisoners watching shadows dance upon the wall of a cave, unable to turn our heads, and unaware of the reality that casts the shadows.

As well as accepting our own weakness, we have to bear patiently with the failings of others. For the first few months living at Elm Grove I was quite overwhelmed by the levels of emotion I felt. I quickly discovered a deep residual anger: a place of rock-solid resentment within. Before moving to Elm Grove, I remember being struck with particular force by one line from Jean Vanier: 'If we come into community without knowing that the reason we come is to discover the mystery of forgiveness, we will soon be disappointed'.[4] What a shock this was to read. I wanted community to be about something else, something bigger or more exciting. But of course, this is the biggest thing there is: this is the nature of God's love. And it's a lifetime's work to embrace.

'SHOW ME, LORD, YOUR WAY' (PS. 85[86].11)

I've spent years grappling with the question of whether I'm called to the monastic life. One of the difficulties at first was my strong instinct that I couldn't possibly be called to enclosed life. While enclosure holds some appeal – the wholeheartedness of it and the freedom to focus one's whole self on God in prayer and the liturgy – I feel a more insistent call to be available to people in the world. Hospitality is a key value in the monastic life, following Benedict's exhortation to welcome people as Christ. Living as a community in an urban setting has meant being accessible to people who are often in particular need, meeting Christ in those whose lives are broken, lonely or burdensome. I feel an urgent call to be near people on the margins, and our experience at Elm Grove – through projects in the local community and working as an assistant chaplain in a school – has opened my eyes to the need of so many to belong, to be listened to and loved, and to have their human dignity restored. People are increasingly thirsting for a real experience of community and an encounter with Christ in prayer.

Contacts with new monastic communities across Europe like Taizé and, more recently, Bose in Northern Italy, have also deeply inspired me and I feel certain we have a lot to learn from their approach: a clear sighted focus on the

Gospel, the return to the roots of monasticism without being overburdened by the weight of centuries of tradition, a fresh awareness of the needs of our world today and the signs of the times. Since this attraction to monastic life was first awakened I've explored the question of whether there's room for a new expression of the monastic impulse in this country too. I have a deep resonance with the idea of an urban monasticism, creating a sanctuary in the city that acts as a visible witness to the coming of the Kingdom.

Another significant part of the puzzle of vocation is a terror of living without an intimate relationship with one other human being. Not marrying seems a huge obstacle that I've battled to overcome. More recently, though, I've realized this is not something I can suppress or heroically carry as my cross. I must give it room to be explored. But it does feel a bit like being torn in two. On the one hand, married love makes so much sense to me as a means of growing towards union with God: it is a sacramental expression of that union we are destined for. But on the other hand, I yearn for the freedom of an exclusive relationship with Christ, an all-consuming love of God which seems to be offered by consecrated life. There is a danger of developing a disembodied spirituality, lacking integration. It must, however, be possible to live a fully embodied life without a sexual relationship: Christ did, but I haven't discovered how yet.

Limiting the options is never easy, and I suspect I'm quite fearful of closing doors, even though it's necessary to close some in order to open others. Making choices is increasingly difficult for contemporary people: we live in a society with so much choice that we are often left paralyzed. Jesus talks of the narrow gate, an image St Benedict understands as significant for the monastic. Benedict warns us not to fear the road that leads to salvation as it is 'bound to be narrow at the outset' (*RB*, Prologue, 48). And where does it lead? If I listen to my fears, I see this gate merely as death, and fail to see beyond to the promise of new life. It may be symptomatic of youth or the outlook of my generation, but I don't think we live with much sense of hope. Many of us fear the future, anxious that all it may hold is the diminishment of life and joy. At moments the Christian life – and especially its monastic expression – looks to me as if it's wholly about renunciation and loss, almost a negation of all that is good or enjoyable. I fail to see the Resurrection through the Cross. I was struck by Pope Benedict's words in his inaugural Mass, when he reminded us of John Paul II's words: 'Do not be afraid! Open wide the doors for Christ!' Pope Benedict went on to say:

> Are we not perhaps all afraid in some way? If we let Christ enter fully into our lives, if we open ourselves totally to Him, are we not afraid that He might take something away from us? Are we not perhaps afraid to give up something significant, something unique, something that makes life so beautiful? Do we not then risk ending up diminished and deprived of our freedom?

And once again the Pope said:

> No! If we let Christ into our lives, we lose nothing, nothing, absolutely nothing of what makes life free, beautiful and great. No! Only in this friendship are the doors of life opened wide. Only in this friendship is the great potential of human existence truly revealed. Only in this friendship do we experience beauty and liberation. And so, today, with great strength and great conviction, on the basis of long personal

experience of life, I say to you, dear young people: Do not be afraid of Christ! He takes nothing away, and He gives you everything.

What a struggle I find it to believe this message. I always find a way to keep something for myself as a back-up plan! We are called again to trust, and in taking the narrow way we will, this side of eternity, 'run on the path of God's commandments, our hearts overflowing with the inexpressible delight of love' (*RB*, Prologue, 49). Joy is promised.

So my journey continues. I am tentatively feeling a way forward in the dark. Over the last five years, I've strained quite a lot for certainty about my future, to know the way ahead. But I've learned it doesn't work like that. We don't know the particulars of where we will be led if we say 'yes' to Christ. He invites us to say 'I will follow you' before we know where he is heading. The monastic life is a kind of experiment in trust. In fact, to take any form of vows – especially in today's world – involves leaping off a cliff into the unknown. Vows are permanent and lifelong, yet who knows who any of us will be in ten years time, or how we may have changed? It is an act of fidelity that goes against the grain, signalling to the world that God is true and faithful. One of the Sunday morning psalms from the Divine Office repeats the cry of joy and triumph, 'His love endures forever'. Rooting my life in the Resurrection, I seek to say with my whole will:

'I shall not die, I shall live
and recount his deeds.' (Ps. 117[118].17)

NOTES

1. J. H. Newman, 'The Pillar of the Cloud'.
2. The psalm numbering here, and throughout the book, is

taken from *The Grail Psalter* which follows the Greek
Septuagint numeration and is, therefore, usually one behind
that of the Vulgate which is given in brackets.
3. St Augustine, *Confessions*, XII.10.
4. J. Vanier (1979), *Community and Growth*. London: Darton,
Longman & Todd, p. 16.

A Slow Boat to China

Michael G. Brunner

There is a saying: 'Pursue knowledge, even if you have to walk all the way to China to find it.' China is merely a metaphor for the lengths one often has to go in order to find Truth, which is one of the names of God. For you, the destination may be India, Iraq, or much closer to home. But for us all, the furthest reaches of China lie deep inside ourselves.

ON CHOOSING A BOAT

'Where do you think I'd fit in?'

Here I was, a 43-year-old ex-Catholic, ex-Muslim, ex-radical, ex-just about anything I'd ever been, now a Catholic again, planning another radical change in my life, one full of experiences but ultimately empty. But in the emptiness there was always the patient, persistent, soft voice of God, saying, 'Here I am; come closer, explore the emptiness.' Sitting across from me was a former classmate, the vocations director of the religious order I had left 23 years before. 'Well, you know all about us,' he said. 'The Dominicans would be good for you, or maybe the Franciscans.'

I knew I needed a community. I had lived my whole life

for myself. A strong community could get me past that, but I didn't know much about communities, so had turned to this friend inside the business for advice. The Dominicans, I thought, had been too involved in the Inquisition, and perhaps they hadn't quite gotten past that. But the Franciscans ... who didn't like St Francis? He liked animals, I liked animals; this might be a good fit. But since this was my chance to get some insight into all the options, I asked, 'What about the Benedictines?' The office we were sitting in was two blocks away from a Benedictine monastery. Without any hesitation, he replied, 'Oh no. You wouldn't like them at all. Not for you ... too many rules.'

'Good', I thought, 'I like a challenge.' And so on my way home I stopped off at a bookstore and purchased the ominously titled *Rule of Saint Benedict.*

CURRENTS IN THE WATER

The person we become is largely formed in our childhood, and, looking back, I can see there the foreshadowing and prediction of the route my life would take: a deep awareness of God; an acute social conscience (I wanted to grow up quickly so that I could be a freedom fighter in Algeria); a passion for progress and change, and a need to break away from the commonplace and leap into the 'ever-rolling stream' of my time, to commit my life to something. As long as I can remember (and that is back to the age of 3 in 1953), my life has been a conversation with God, sometimes quiet, sometimes loud, sometimes joyful, other times sad, and for a time, angry and argumentative, even when I was in the midst of sin. I have been blessed with a wonderful family, sound health and a good mind, and for all this I have always been most thankful to God.

30

Our family home in Rochester, upper New York State, was across the street from a large park with a public swimming pool. Each day in the summer for many years my mother would walk me over early in the morning for swimming lessons. I never, ever, learned how to swim, nor even float. This was a source of shame to me. When I was 12, I went on a camping trip with a friend and his family up into the Adirondack mountains. We camped alongside a lake where I would safely paddle about on an air-raft. One day, I paddled out into the middle of the lake, got off the raft and began to tread water. (Somehow I had learned to tread water.) I determined then that I would swim, so I picked up the air-raft and threw it as far as I could, about 15 feet. I was there, alone, and if I wanted to live, I would have to swim. I did!

At 16, I began to volunteer at an inner-city social centre and was shocked that people could live in such dire poverty just a few miles from my affluent neighbourhood. Enraged that these people were so despised by many of my friends and neighbours, I became consumed with indignation: this *must* be the mission of the Church. I read every book on civil rights, the class struggle; I marched in marches, spoke out and led a group of seminarians in a downtown youth project, brought together groups of inner-city youngsters and young people from my own parish. My last semester in high school was a time of restless anticipation and upheaval. We expected the Vietnam War would end soon, but instead, the lives of Martin Luther King and Robert F. Kennedy ended. In August the Soviet Union invaded Czechoslovakia. The world seemed in deep, deep trouble.

To make an impact in civil rights, this moral cause of the age, I joined the Josephite Fathers in 1968, and enrolled at Epiphany College in Newburgh, New York. I had never lived in such a restrictive environment, one which brought

31

out a cynical streak in me. But I adjusted, making some good friendships which persist to this day. The novitiate came after two years of college and was located in an isolated, small town in Delaware. There was very little structured activity other than cooking and common prayer, but the novice master was one of the holiest (and happiest) men I have ever met, obviously in touch with God, and who knew what the priesthood was all about; his example was the greatest teaching. We novices, however, were all going 'stir-crazy' in our own way, and we quickly got on each other's nerves. The novitiate did not guide us in how to live in community, but I still made my profession at the age of 21.

WATERSHED

The summer after taking vows was a watershed. Not having heard from my best friend who was one year ahead of me and working at a parish in Baltimore, I went to the major seminary in Washington and was stunned to learn that my friend was to be married in just over a week. I spent two days with him talking about this radical change. Celibacy was not for him. Because he had been my philosophical anchor for three years, I was now challenged to cut loose and find the depths of my own commitment. I reached a crisis and began to challenge tenets of faith, such as the Real Presence of Christ in the Eucharist, the Trinity and so on. I really could find no meaning in the religion I had taken for granted all my life. I felt inadequate to help people with life problems in the social apostolate (such as unemployment, poverty, marital strife) since it seemed to me that I'd never had a problem that wasn't a figment of my imagination. And I had also discovered my sexuality. I was truly challenged at this point. It was my first real problem, although I didn't realize it. But since I doubted my faith

32

and its relevance, doubted myself and my abilities, and saw
no way to assuage my raging hormones, I asked for a leave
of absence. This was denied, so I left.

Suddenly I was just me and I didn't know who I was,
what I wanted to do or what I really believed.

A NEW ROUTE

During this period of spiritual disillusionment, I investigated
Islam. I found there answers to my doubts and problems with
Catholicism, and the simplicity of Islam provided a foundation upon which to rebuild my faith. I studied assiduously,
including the Arabic language. I was very much impressed
with the difference Islam had made in the lives of many Black
Americans, with the sincerity of their faith and in the
tremendous transformation in their lives. Islam was simple
and direct, gave rules for life, and like monasticism, revolved
around five regular daily times of prayer. I learned to love this
prayer and God sustained me in this simple faith until I was
ready to move on. I became active at the National Islamic
Center in Washington, giving tours and expositions on Islam.
There I was asked what Muslim name I would take. I became
bogged down looking through the 99 attributes or names of
God, the names of the prophets and other traditional Muslim
names, and was unable to choose, so the brothers named me
Abdullah, meaning 'servant of God', to which I added
Abdur-Rashid, meaning 'servant of the wise and righteous
guide'. In my prayer at that time I was asking God for the gift
of wisdom, and for the ability to renounce the pursuit of
wealth and power. In reading the traditions of Muhammad, I
was struck by one which I have since pored over constantly in
my life in order to seek its meaning at any given moment, a
meaning which is always deepening: 'The greatest struggle',
said Muhammad, 'is against the self'.

TROUBLE EN ROUTE

The self is unruly.

   The hotel in Washington DC where I'd taken my first job
and had been precipitately promoted to general manager by
the age of 23 became a crucible. I was far too naïve to
supervise a lot of people and deal with the sharks of business.
I can't believe how patient the owners were with me and
how they taught me. Eventually, they brought in an
experienced manager. When the oil embargo and recession
hit, they let me go. I was crushed and tasted failure for the
first time. My father said I was fortunate to have that
happen early in life, which remark I did not appreciate at
the time. Thus I was unemployed for three months. Not
having a job is a terrible thing. In our culture a job identifies
you and calculates your social worth. While I got a lot of
rest, it was maddening. I became more involved at the
Islamic Center, prayed and studied more but also night-
clubbed a lot. Life was very empty without a job. I was
finally employed by a big hotel where I learned and worked
voraciously. I loved it, but was having to work that job *and* a
part-time job to make ends meet. Whenever I could, I
travelled to New York City where I had made many friends:
I was becoming infatuated with New York, the Big Apple.
My genius brother then arrived back in New York to teach
at Columbia University. Since I then knew I would have a
place to live, I quit my job, sold my furniture and moved to
Manhattan.

   One impetus for moving to New York was to make it big
in the hotel business by working at the Waldorf Astoria
Hotel. I did not even know where it was. But I knew that it
was a Hilton Hotel. So, the Monday after I moved, I went
to the New York Hilton, planning to submit an application
and then request directions to the Waldorf. I never made it

34

to the Waldorf because they hired me immediately, thanks to the fact the word 'credit' appeared once in my resumé. Never underestimate the power of a word. I am amazed when I look back. I left everything to go to New York, had no prospects nor connections for a job and yet was hired at the first place I went on my first business day in the city. But back then, I knew it would happen that way, like throwing the air-raft and swimming. This became a useful life-skill.

In New York, I lost touch with organized Islam. No longer able to make the Friday prayers, I did continue to read, study and pray. Muslim books were much more available in New York and for the first time I read the works of the Sufi spiritual masters. In my life God has always worked very slowly, even when I was going fast. I read the Sufi works but I did not understand them. Yet I remembered what I could not understand and thrashed these puzzlements about in my mind periodically and slowly began to grow into them; when I *had* grown into them, I was back at Catholicism and Christ, but that is jumping ahead in the story. I did acquire here an anchor, a $3 stainless steel bracelet (which I ultimately gave to a Jewish student on his Bar Mitzvah) inscribed with the Arabic words, 'Help from God and victory is near'.

New York taught me how to say 'no'. You had to say no in New York, or you'd be made mincemeat. What a place to live! The music and nightlife were wonderful and non-stop, but people were cold and cunning; excess was everywhere and egos were paramount. Personal relationships were disappointing, to say the least. I said I would stay until I felt like I was becoming a New Yorker and then I would leave.

A WARM SOUTHERN PORT

In 1979 the hotel was sold. The corporation wanted to move me to Washington, much to my delight. My boss vetoed that. Next the corporation wanted me to go to Miami Beach. That was much more to my delight and more money. Again that was vetoed. My boss offered me a job at the Waldorf, much to my amazement. Just what I had come to New York dying for was handed me on a silver platter when all I wanted to do was leave. I always use my 'Waldorf' experience now as a metaphor for seductive temptation. My 'godfather' in the corporation advised me to resign and come to Miami, where I would be re-hired with no penalty. So I resigned, telling everyone I was off to Egypt to study, and flew straight to Miami and my new job.

Most of us who moved down to Miami for the corporation came to detest the place. All but two left after a year or two. I attempted to put down roots in the Muslim community, but they were a close-knit group, not welcoming of outsiders. Organized Islam was now turning me off. After the experience with the Muslim brotherhood, and the Muslim revolution-gone-awry in Iran, I clearly saw that scandal was not at all limited to Christianity and that hypocrisy was not a sin of Catholics only.

Six months later, after attending my brother's wedding, I determined that it was time to pick up the air-raft and give it a good heave again. I simply could not stay there. Nothing provokes the process of discovery like discomfort; I was drinking very heavily, though not, at least at that time, so as to affect my job or health. Years before, my father had explained to me that every man has a breaking point, and that I must be conscious of my limitations; I knew I was approaching mine.

The pain and isolation of Miami forced me to look deeply and honestly within myself. I discovered the works of Joseph Campbell, who identified God as 'Sat-Chit-Ananda' (Being-Thought-Bliss) and famously advised, 'Follow your bliss'. He tied together the threads of the spiritual and the here-

and-now in my consciousness. I began reading with a better understanding of my conviction that 'God is one'. I discovered that much of my unhappiness was due to my life's selfish direction. My 'bliss' was clearly not in the pursuit of a lucrative career in a glamorous business. I felt no meaning or purpose in simply protecting the assets of a corporation. I did not know exactly where my bliss was nor what I wanted to do, but I knew this wasn't it. Because of the circumstances of my coming to Miami, I did not want to ask for a transfer and did not particularly care if I had to scrub floors, as long as it was 'back home' in Washington. A friend there offered me a place to stay, so, with great joy, I submitted my resignation. As I turned it in, I was told my new mentor had just been transferred to Washington. He called me, as did other corporate friends who heard I was leaving. They offered a job in Washington; I declined. Then the calls became more insistent, implying I had a moral obligation to help because of what they had done for me. It was rather like the 'Waldorf' scenario, but this time I accepted, although I said I would only work for them for one year.

I came back self-confident, arrogant, much in demand socially and I quickly forgot about the one-year idea, plunging into my job and a whirlwind social life. It was the 1980s and the Ronald Reagan culture was a powerful drug. I fell happily into a comfortable life of self-indulgence.

A ROUGH GUIDE

I would hate to think how I would have been had I not been praying during this time. Muhammad said, 'The five daily prayers are like a stream in which you bathe; if you wash five times daily, you will be clean.' On the other hand, as Albert Speer said, 'It is hard to recognize the devil when he has his hand on your shoulder', fulfilling your desires. God truly kept me from self-destruction – just. One day in 1981, I was walking home from a friend's where we had been drinking and smoking. I became convinced I was having a heart attack, was disoriented and walked all the way home in the searing heat of the Washington summer. By the time I got home I felt I was dying. I spent the weekend in bed and went to the doctor on the Monday. He attributed it all to stress and simply prescribed five milligrams of Valium daily.

I was happy that I wasn't dying, but it was brought home to me that someday I would. Until then I had dealt with death by avoidance, refusing to attend funerals or wakes. I realized that death would be quite inopportune under my present circumstances. My life would not have been missed by many, nor did I think I had made the type of contribution to life of which I was capable. The Gospel Parable of the Talents came to me, and I realized that I had not only buried what I had been given, but that I had even forgotten where. I resolved to pray more and delved into the works of the Sufis more seriously: Al-Ghazali's *Ihya Ulum-ud-Din* and *The Alchemy of Happiness*; Rumi's *Diwan Shams-i-Tabriz* and *Mathnawi*; Hakim Sana'i's *The Walled Garden of Truth*; Attar's *Conference of the Birds*; and Al Jilani's *Revelations of the Unseen*. The sign of the Sufi is the winged heart, and the way of the Sufi is love of God, and the goal of the Sufi is the annihilation of the illusory self in the love of God. This was all very simply what Christ taught; I saw that I had fled Christianity and Christ because it demanded the death of the unbridled self in the face of our self-idolizing culture. Orthodox Islam was clouded by legalism which led me to believe that, as long as the laws were observed, the self could reign. Yet the Sufis teach that the idols set up against God today are in men's hearts: wealth, sex, power – the very passions of the self.

The way was so much the same as the Christian way. The only thing missing was the apprehensible reality of God's love for us and to us, Jesus Christ, and the sure promise of eternal life through Redemption and the Resurrection. I was coming close, but I had not yet the courage to accept Christ back into my life; I continued to rationalize him away.

LEARNING NOT TO ROCK THE BOAT
BEFORE BOARDING

There now occurred an event which may seem trivial but which made possible the rest of my life. I consider it my greatest personal accomplishment ... Ever since high school, I had been smoking cigarettes. In my last two college years, when working full-time and taking full-time classes, I began smoking heavily and, by the time I graduated, was hopelessly addicted and smoking three packs of cigarettes per day. When pinched for money, I would buy cigarettes before I would buy food. I had tried countless times to stop, without success. On 10 September 1987 I had my last cigarette and when I had gone a year smoke-free, was a new man. Words cannot convey what it means to be free of an addiction, albeit a legal one, free of something which controlled your life and over which you had no control, something against which you had failed countless times. I cannot imagine what hell drug addicts go through. After I gave up cigarettes, I knew I could really do a lot of the hard things in life I had been avoiding. I knew I could take control of, or at least responsibility for, the direction of my life. The experience gives me some hint of what the Resurrection really means. There was no rational reason for my success this time; it was a gift of grace, which opened up a future of new possibilities. Indeed, if at first you don't succeed, try again!

39

After this my career took off. I was given responsibility for a group of hotels. For the first time I felt like I was succeeding when I was. I had to admit to myself that this relentless pursuit of success in business was not because that was what I wanted to do, but because I had been shaken by the failure of my first managerial stint in my twenties and had to prove to myself that I could do it right. I also realized, as I had years before, that I wanted to do more than just spend my life making money for someone else or even myself. My new company culture had made me more respectful of money, but I was a socialist at heart. Since real estate was the watchword of the 'go-go' 1980s, I bought property. In *Gone with the Wind*, Mr O'Hara soberly admonishes Scarlett, 'Land is everything'. It does change your way of thinking and can cut two ways. One way is positive and is akin to the Benedictine vow of stability: it situates your home in this world in a particular neighbourhood and town to which you belong, establishing a place of belonging, to which your loyalty, time, attention and resources are ordered. It stabilizes one's life. The other way is akin to rampant capitalism, putting property before people. This was a real lesson. My wise father always said 'Do not encumber yourself with "stuff"'. Well, the house was 'stuff' and meant a second full-time job in order to care for it. It did reinforce discipline and responsibility, but I was happy to sell it off when preparing for another heave of the air-raft.

GOD SENDS A BEACON

Each year for Christmas I would drive up to Rochester, New York, to be with my family. The drive goes along the Susquehanna River and through the mountains of Pennsylvania and the southern tier of New York State. I always looked forward to these seven-hour drives as times to be alone, to apprehend the natural beauty along the way and generally to lean back into the arms of God. In 1988 this turned out to be a special trip, the road to Damascus, I call it. As I was listening to Christmas carols, out of the blue the question came to me clearly and insistently: 'Who do you say Jesus Christ really is?' He whom I had been putting out of my mind and rationalizing away for 20 years. It is difficult to explain, but my life and spiritual growth had reached critical mass and the answer first came as a cascade of connections and then an explosion of love and faith. God from God. In an affective way, I identified with the Prodigal Son. Two decades earlier I had written a poem to 'You whom I call God' which was accusatory in tone. I wrote then: 'What have you saved me from? What difference has Jesus Christ made in the world?' My conclusion then was 'nothing'. From the vantage point of an additional 20 years and a better understanding of sin, I understood things differently: the phrase from the Gospel 'The kingdom of God is within you' (Lk. 17.21 AV) had real meaning.

For the first 21 years of my life I had studied Catholicism unquestioningly, without real understanding, the same way I memorized trigonometric formulae (which God knows I never understood). Then, thirsting for understanding, I studied Islam, and recall readily many passages of the Qur'an, traditions of Muhammad and lessons of Islamic saints which I understood and incorporated into my life. In my process of learning I would mentally cross-reference these with Christian parallels, but because understanding of so many things came to me through the door of Islam, the Islamic words often come to mind. I feel self-conscious about this now as a Christian, but as God would have it, I would not be here if I had not been there.

The great foundation of Islam is the unity of God;

Teilhard de Chardin's main message is the unity of Creation in Christ. I affectively understood the mystery of the Trinity, which in no way detracts from the unity. Making these connections was wonderful stuff, but I had been used to practising my faith in the privacy of my mind and in prayer, allowing bits and pieces to spill over into my active life. I had been separated from the community of faith. Muhammad said, 'He who removes himself but a hand's breadth from the community is lost.' I did not feel lost, but I knew I had come close. Yet I was still distrustful of the institutional Church; I thought it was enough to have accepted Christ along the road.

The Qur'an says, 'If you take but one step toward God, he will take ten steps toward you.' In that drive to Rochester it had occurred to me that the reason I had been so dissatisfied with my life was that I had been running from the religious vocation I had once pursued. I reasoned that this was kind of ridiculous at my age and attempted to put the idea out of my mind. What did come to the forefront of my mind was the Qur'anic concept of the *mizan*, the balance of life. I realized that my life was now almost evenly balanced between years of belief and service to God and years of selfish struggle; I was approaching the point from which the meaning of my life would be determined on the *mizan*. I knew which direction I wanted to take, but not which road: another concept from 'The Lord's Prayer' of Islam, 'Guide us along the straight path, the path of those who incur Your favour, not the path of those who earn Your anger, nor the path of those who go astray.' The path that kept appearing in my mind was the priesthood. I felt that it would do no harm to reinvestigate the Church.

THIS WAY TO CHINA

I had, in fact, just met a former Carmelite who was youth minister at the Catholic church three blocks away from my house, so I went to attend Sunday Mass, slipping into the back pew, just in case I had to beat a hasty retreat. My only impression of that day was that I was disappointed by the homily which was entirely about a business matter which was preoccupying the parish – I'd wanted to be edified. However, I was touched enough to return the following Sunday and was greatly moved by the Mass, the priest and the homily; this was a Church of the winged heart. It was a 'united nations' of parishioners: 50 per cent immigrants of 100 different nationalities, 25 per cent White Americans and 25 per cent Black Americans. I began attending regularly, always sitting in the back pew.

During this time the young assistant priest at my church preached a homily in which he related his experience as a young child climbing a tree. He had climbed too high and could not get down. His father came and stood beneath him and told him not to worry and to jump down, and he would catch him in his arms. The little boy was as afraid to jump as to climb down, but eventually jumped into his father's arms. We needed to have enough faith, Fr Patrick said, to let go and jump into the arms of God. This had a great effect upon me. I would put myself in God's hands. I gradually became more active in the Church. I first determined to help with what was the least popular activity but critical for the parish, that is, bingo, and then was asked to assist as an usher.

The five daily prayers are one of the great pillars of Islam. At all hours of the day, somewhere, believers are turning toward Mecca, the site of Abraham's temple, and praying to God. As the earth rotates, the prayers ripple across its face

43

like a series of waves, giving constant praise to God. I recalled that the Church's cosmic wave of praise was the Divine Office, as we prayed it in the novitiate, and so I went to the Newman Book Store to pick up a volume of *Christian Prayer* and the *Office of Readings* which I began to pray again. I accelerated my activity in the parish and became a lector. While all this was going on, I was feeling more wholesome than I ever had, embracing celibacy, giving up the bad habits of a lifetime, and my career was doing just fine. I just could not shake the notion of a vocation; it was gnawing at me. I had begun to question again the purpose of my life. How could I, with all my experiences, mistakes made and lessons learned, be of any benefit to anyone else?

THE BOAT AND OTHER OPTIONS

It was at this point that I visited my former classmate with whom I began this story. I told him about my thoughts, thinking he would disabuse me of this silly notion. He did not. I reviewed my spiritual journey with him and he gave me guidance and even encouragement. After our first meeting, I thought I should get a second opinion. A classmate of mine, who had been one of my best friends in high school, is a Discalced Carmelite and was then stationed in Washington. As I was re-approaching the Church I had re-established contact with him and he helped the process along. I told him that I was thinking about a vocation; 'I thought so', he said, and also encouraged me, while admonishing me to test myself lest my impulses simply be the fiery glow of re-conversion. I knew the real test would be time. Would I be faithful, would the 'glow' last?

While I had come to know and acknowledge sin, I did not believe in Satan, the obstacle and force opposing God. Yet in analysing my past life, I saw the effects of this unseen hand. As I was now determining a new positive direction, I was amazed to see temptation and negative forces rise up at every turn to dissuade me. Suddenly I was in great social demand: anyone I so much as cast a glance at wanted to hop into bed with me; my job was going so well I was tempted with power and a change of direction. Whatever was desirable and would get in the way of a religious life was mine for the asking. That's why the 'Waldorf' metaphor means so much to me now. At the onset of all this, I saw the movie *The Last Temptation of Christ* which was so scorned. I was quite moved by the central thesis and understood much more the humanity of Christ and how empathetic Christ was with my condition. As it always has, prayer sustained me.

When I was very young, I was given a children's Bible in story form. Two Old Testament stories were for some reason burned into my mind: one is the call of the young Samuel, 'Here I am, Lord'; the other is of Moses in prayer, arms upheld by Aaron and Hur, the tide of battle ebbing and flowing with his constancy. These images would be particularly relevant in the next stage of the journey.

Everything which I thought would prove I didn't have a vocation and was an obstacle seemed to be vanishing, one of the biggest ones being the sale of the house and settlement of debts. I knew the clock was ticking and I had better make some choices. I started getting occasional informal spiritual direction from my assistant priest and began looking for a community. All the communities I looked into, however, seemed like men off on their own missions, and, above all, with no common prayer life. Everything seemed to be pointing to this group which I had been warned against, the Benedictines. So I read the *Rule of St Benedict*. I was quite impressed, and relieved that there was no mandatory flagellation or anything else I wouldn't be up to. This was real community, perhaps the sort which I'd always been seeking, and was a working rule, exactly analogous to the way of the Sufi masters. Was this where I was being led?

I sent off a barrage of enquiries, not knowing where to start, but right away the reply from St Louis Abbey, Missouri, stood out and spoke to me ... 'Bound for freedom'. The Franciscans and others also spoke ... 'No'. Loving animals didn't help at all. I then waited a while. During this time I was reading *The Cloud of Unknowing* and the writings of Hildegard of Bingen, Meister Eckhart, and Abhishiktananda, a Benedictine living in India who wove together the threads of Eastern and Western prayer traditions. The call seemed to me louder than ever and I determined to answer.

One day I was called upon by our parish Director of Religious Education who asked me to speak at a 'rap session' on Islam. It was the first time I'd told my story to anyone other than a priest, and the first time I tied together a lot of the threads that make up this narrative. It reinforced my conviction that deep down people want guidance with spiritual problems more than anything else, and that I could contribute more, love more, in that way, more so than in social matters.

So I took the plunge and visited St Louis.

The monastic life appealed to me because it is the freedom to live and work in the love of God, it is centred upon prayer, its work *is* prayer and it is supported by community, which provides the strength to persist, the roots from which to grow in love and service. I have learned in life that the most important, most significant contributions are the personal ones: the positive influence one life has upon another, the words whispered in the ear, the lesson lived rather than delineated; and the more centred the source of the contribution, the greater the effect. I see monks contributing to life in this way, as powerful transmitters of God's love and care and as living signs of contradiction – as the cross of Christ is – to the world, showing people the way home to God.

WELCOME ABOARD ... THE RIGHT BOAT

So, St Louis accepted me despite all my baggage, which was too heavy for most Orders for whom I was either too old or too strange. Benedictines are good at that.

Anyone 'in the know' about Benedictines (which I was not) knows that monks and monasteries are famous for their hospitality. So a Benedictine monastery was quite appropriate for a career person in the hospitality industry. St Benedict's *Rule* is quite explicit. You must regard the guest as Christ and treat him or her accordingly.

It is an amazing thing to experience from other human beings what we hope to experience from God, complete acceptance and respect. I had been used to *giving* hospitality, not only to paying guests in my hotels but also by accepting others who were radically different ... poor, African, Muslim, for example, into my life and to identifying with them. But to be accepted and identified with when *you* are the different one is equally blessed and grace-filled. It is humbling (in the best sense of that word) and transformative. It enables one (in a phrase from a poem I wrote years ago) 'to live forever already'. God is one, and yet God is a community of three distinct persons; and so God's life and bliss encompass the multiplicity of humanity. God is divine hospitality.

In the spring of 1994 I was accepted for that August as a postulant in the English Benedictine Congregation community of St Louis Abbey, Missouri. Founded from Ampleforth Abbey, England in 1955, the community became an independent house in 1973 and includes among its works a large parish and a school. I looked forward eagerly to beginning this new life, but also with some anxiety. Sometime in this period I had a vivid dream in which, vested as a cleric, I was processing down the main aisle of a church toward one of those old ornate gothic pulpits. When I came to the base of the pulpit a black man emerged from the congregation, put a headlock on me and pulled me to the floor where he put his face up to mine and sternly warned me, 'Don't forget us.' What could that mean? Was I making the wrong choice to enter a community serving an affluent white population? This would bother me for the next two years.

When speaking about my doubts to an old friend from my wildest days in New York, I said of the monks, 'They're so English, so stuffy, so rigid, so conservative.' My friend burst into laughter and said, 'So are you!' That was a revelation; the truth will set you free. So I joyfully sold off and disbursed my assets and 'retired' on 30 June. In early July I took a six-week train journey, which I call my Farewell Tour, around the United States.

In August 1994 I arrived at the Abbey as a long-term guest, which state leads to postulancy. In this state one lives the life of a monk but doesn't have much to do. This lack of activity was a constant irritant to me, but I realized that I had to make a transition from a 'go-go' executive and businessman to something more tranquil. How did I cope? On a superficial level, but one which I felt keenly, I was annoyed by the geographical disorientation: I knew I was in St Louis, but I didn't know landmarks, streets, suburbs or sections of the city. Any conversation, statement or news item that dealt with location was totally beyond my comprehension. Time would take care of that, but that annoyance was symptomatic of experiencing a loss of control; I was no longer the boss. Since I had lived by myself, silence in verbal communication was not a problem, but I had been used to living surrounded by music and TV movies and news, so that took some adjustment. In all the new demands I found that channelling my displaced energy into the realities of my new situation helped resolve irritations and conflicts. (This is a very ancient Buddhist practice, 'right concentration'.) The monastery has beautiful, spacious grounds and simply to walk and apprehend nature (for me especially the birds) was both calming, constructive spiritually and prayerful, and so were running on the track and working out in the school's weight room.

Learning how to read again, not 'speed reading' for practical information, but *lectio divina* and more leisurely reading for appreciation and understanding was a great gift. And following my natural curiosity to learn all the monastic *arcana* I could was another outlet. Trying to do my best in the sacristy jobs I had, polishing silver, cleaning up candle wax, setting up for liturgies, also helped ... although it made cleaning up candle wax seem more important to me than it objectively is. The biggest help in adjustment was, however, the understanding, sympathy and help of the monks, all of whom had been through the same thing before me. All of this was working, and after a few weeks I felt quite at home reading, praying and working in this revolutionary new way of life.

After Christmas, however, I took a nosedive. I only learned later that I suffer from seasonal depression, but in the throes of it I left and returned to Washington. But I stayed in touch with the Abbey and when spring came, I knew I had made a mistake in leaving. Consequently, on a visit to the Abbey I was invited to accept the position of youth minister at the Abbey's parish in St Louis. And so I began there again in August 1996.

I grew tremendously, spiritually and intellectually. But my life was different from most of the monks: the parish worked on a different rhythm. My involvement revived some of my doubts about working with the affluent. (I still had a lot to learn.) At the same time I was manipulated by a friend into loaning him large sums of money from my lines of credit. He was unable to repay, which made it impossible for me to enter the novitiate. It seemed best to return to Washington to settle the debts. There God also blessed me with the opportunity to work in my old parish, which had so skilfully led me back to the heart of the Church.

Finally, in August 1997, I entered the novitiate and never looked back.

No one suffered more consternation than I at these false starts. I knew all along this was a test of my resolve and moral fibre. In the end I gave it to God and trusted his will to work it out. I'd been impressed by the story of someone asking a monk, 'What do you do in the monastery?' The monk replied, 'We fall and get up, we fall and get up.'

This is my only expectation in monastic life. To continue my journey toward God with the help of my brothers, falling and getting up again, helping them as well, contributing to the community life and work, falling and getting up in that too. The way of obedience to the abbot is a way of purification, the refiner's fire; I know that fire burns, but I have seen the results too, especially in the older monks, and they are worth it.

It is within community that I found the answer to the question, 'For what purpose is my life?' It is within the life and work of the community that my past experiences, mistakes made and lessons learned, bear fruit for the good of others. It is within the Benedictine monastery in slow-paced middle America, following the *Rule of Saint Benedict*, that I have become the genuine socialist revolutionary I always wanted to be, living a counter-cultural existence in radical freedom to love God and others. This is not always easy. I know that I will be tempted to go back to a more comfortable existence, to self-indulgent pleasures, as I am tempted even now to find a comfortable career and indulge in sinful pleasures I once tasted. Temptations even morph and although one is never tempted beyond one's strength, as I have become stronger in my faith and conviction, I have seen the temptations change: some 'Waldorf' always looms out from a fog-shrouded, seemingly near but distant shore.

EPILOGUE: TO CHINA ...

Columbus set out for, and at first thought he had reached, India. He soon learned the truth. I am under no illusion that my monastery is China, just a boat that will surely get me there. So here I am, searching, falling and getting up, on this strange, unmarked, watery route along which God is still leading me in this monastic community.

It was a challenge going back to school, but I loved it.

It was a challenge to start teaching high-school boys, but I love it.

It was a tremendous challenge to become a priest, but I love it.

It was a challenge to become headmaster, but I'm learning to love it.

No doubt there will be other challenges, but God will show the way to navigate them.

China is always just over the horizon, but on a slow boat you grow and learn. And in the fullness of time, you will arrive.

3

'A Tune Beyond Us, Yet Ourselves'[1]

Laurentia Johns

The sound of a bell, the swish of fabric, and a cloud of incense: I was completely trapped. I had only braved the church to look at the stained-glass windows and instead found myself caught up in what I later learned was 'Benediction', a service which, with its endless repetitions and incantations, did nothing to weaken my suspicions of mumbo-jumbo superstition in the Roman Catholic Church. Yet, almost despite myself, I was gripped by a strong urge to return to the same church for Mass the next day. It was an autumn day in 1986 – a day that changed my life ...

IMPELLED TO ACT

I felt totally at home at Mass: it was like finding something I didn't even know I'd lost. This sense of a home-coming seems to be the universal experience of converts. Interestingly, 'return' is a major theme in the *Rule of St Benedict* (*RB*): in the Prologue we are invited to 'return to him from whom we have strayed', and again at the end of *The Rule*, Benedict asks, 'Are you hastening to your heavenly homeland?' (*RB* 73:8). We are all on a return journey to God.

52

Each subsequent Sunday for several weeks saw me commuting from my Anglican parish Holy Communion service to the Catholic Mass at St David's, Swansea in South Wales. I started attending a discussion group, armed with a battery of arguments against the papacy, the over-predominant position of Mary in Roman Catholic worship and so on. Week by week there was a gradual disarmament by the skilful arguments of Dom Leo Bonsall OSB, the monk leading the sessions (St David's was served by the Benedictine monks of Belmont Abbey, Hereford). Everything he said seemed so reasonable, logical and right that I came to realize how little I'd thought about Anglican doctrine. For the first time, I read the Thirty-Nine Articles, only to discover that I disagreed with several of them, particularly those concerned with Holy Communion. On the positive side, I was fascinated by Dom Leo as a person, admired his commitment as a monk, and was struck by how fully human and alive he seemed. When it came to the collection of names of those wishing to go forward to the Rite of Election (the first stage in the formal process of becoming a Roman Catholic), I felt bound to take that step. I felt quite helpless to refuse, in fact, though I knew it would cause pain in the parish which had been my spiritual home for the previous 22 years.

This was an exciting time but also an unsettling one. Something seemed to be brewing up inside me. Dom Leo, alert to the nature of this unsettled state, made arrangements for me to visit Stanbrook Abbey in February 1987. I was warmly received by the abbess and, rather to my consternation, felt strongly drawn to the life. It was, I think, the singing which attracted me. I experienced what Timothy Radcliffe OP has written of so eloquently, 'that the *Rule of St Benedict* offers a sort of hollow centre ... in which God may live and be glimpsed ... It is the singing of the Office several times a day that shows that this void is filled with the glory of God'.[2] Although I sensed a strong call to be part of that choir and knew, at an intellectual level, that it would allow me, as I most wished, to witness to my faith without having to make a speech or don a sandwich-board, I wasn't ready for that kind of commitment.

I was received into the Roman Catholic Church on Sunday 3 May 1987 at St David's Priory, Swansea, just over six months after the 'Benediction' experience. The feeling was a combination of unspeakable joy, complete rectitude, newness, lightness and utter normality – a melody beyond me, yet my most intimate self.

Each conversion, is, I believe, a gift of the Church (as well as *to* the Church), a discernible result of her continuous, though usually indiscernible action: the Holy Spirit temporarily surfaces. It is, perhaps, such continuity of the Spirit's action (which we tend to perceive as a *dis*continuity in a dramatic conversion) that explains why each step in the conversion process seems so normal and the only thing to do at the time (even though there is, inevitably, some soul-searching on the way). If I were to have drawn up a balance-sheet of sorts, the 'plus' column for St David's would have included the reverence of the people: families genuflecting, lighting candles, knowing themselves to be part of something transcendent. This contrasted with the predominantly female congregation and very sociable atmosphere at the Anglican parish. On the other hand, I did miss Anglican Evensong and the wonderful hymns: there was nothing quite like them in the Catholic churches I attended (even Stanbrook), though I believe hymns have become far more ecumenical since then. I also had a sense that the Catholic Church had a long way to go to catch up on grass-roots involvement in parish/diocesan life, some-thing which had always been a strong feature of the

Anglican system. (Again, I think much has changed in the intervening years with the advent of parish councils in Catholic Churches, for example.) But really, it was not the kind of decision made by a careful weighing of pros and cons. I just felt impelled to act, and only looking back can one begin to detect the strong underwater activities of the Holy Spirit over several decades.

GENESIS & EXODUS

I was baptized on 10 May 1959 at St Michael's (Church in Wales), Llangyfelach, Swansea. My father had been christened in the Church in Wales, though never practised, and had rather a horror of organized religion. Of a philosophical nature, he believed in 'something beyond' and used to repeat a phrase of his mother's (which sounds like Eckhart, though she had never heard of him): 'There is no God. God is Love.' My mother was an orphan and, as far as we knew, had not been baptized as an infant. A nervous person in the early years of their marriage, she would wake up at night terrified of death. My father prescribed 'religion'. I admire him greatly for this, considering his own views. Neither did he ever try to influence us children as far as religion was concerned: my three brothers and sister and I were given complete freedom after being encouraged to attend church up to the time of confirmation. I always had a strong awareness of the presence of God (I think most children do until it is taught out of them by their surroundings). The story is family folklore of how, arriving home from school one day without my 3-year-old brother, I serenely answered my mother's frantic questions as to his whereabouts with, 'God's looking after him.' At 7 I had asked for my own copy of the New Testament which I read avidly at bedtime. I can vividly recall one night, after putting out the light, extending my hand into the dark and asking Jesus to take it. I felt nothing but went to sleep peacefully.

My mother was baptized on Whitsunday, 1970 and I was confirmed with her that same day. We were well prepared for confirmation by our vicar who was my first mentor in prayer. He was ahead of his time, recommending any posture that was comfortable rather than insisting that we kneel, and also suggesting that prayer-time need not necessarily be just before bed. Using the acronym, ACTS (adoration, confession, thanksgiving, supplication) as an outline structure, he encouraged simplicity, openness, confidence and the need to pray daily. Soon I found that missing prayer was like missing a meal and so, with hardly a break, I have prayed each day since I was 10 years old. Fully involved in the parish, my religious leanings were certainly pronounced and unusual among my peers, but in many ways I was a fairly normal teenager, enjoying sport, theatre and a busy social life. At the age of 18 I went up to Oxford but never really found a spiritual home there as the Anglican churches were too evangelical for me. The chapel at my college (St Hugh's) for Evensong and Compline provided a kind of base – intimations of the Benedictine call – but I decided it would be a good opportunity to explore other Christian traditions, not with any thought of changing denomination but simply as part of my broader education. Yet, by the time I'd gone down from Oxford (1980), even church at home no longer seemed as before. I was by then in love with a rather staunch atheist and the next seven years proved to be a turbulent time of personal struggle trying to make this relationship work and preserve my own faith at the same time. The tension almost pulled me apart and very nearly alienated me from the family. I suffered from clinical depression for six months, plumbing the depths of despair.

Somehow, prayer continued and even saved me, though with hindsight, I can see the dangers of personal prayer outside the sacramental life of the Church and without a spiritual guide. There is much scope for self-delusion and the reinforcement of unhealthy behaviour patterns. My own very strong self-will, over self-reliance and a masochistic streak conspired to make me go on trying to make a doomed relationship work, even when it was destructive. But God held on to me and worked through the most constricted of channels, eventually catapulting me out of the relationship, into the Church and, for good measure and my own more sure salvation, into a Benedictine monastery! But that is to get ahead of events.

By the summer of 1986, relieved of the heavy burden of the relationship, I was still somewhat disorientated. It was during this period of not unhappy drifting among the wreckage that I met a man who was planning to enter a monastery quite soon. We spent many hours that summer talking in the car-park attendant's hut where he had a temporary job at one of the local beaches in Swansea. I felt my soul coming back to life in these conversations and saw so clearly the cavernous gap in the previous relationship which hadn't allowed of them. We talked of God, we talked of his vocation to the monastic life, we talked of my happiness at the L'Arche community in France where I'd spent a year after graduating, and the importance of the 'community' aspect of that happiness. My companion's observation that 'you seem to need some kind of community' made me reflect more fully on that time at L'Arche ...

RETROSPECTIVE: A YEAR AT L'ARCHE

My motives for going to L'Arche after coming down from Oxford in the summer of 1980 were far from unmixed and not at all altruistic: I'd been torn between studying French or Geography and, when Geography eventually won, resolved to spend a year in France after graduating. A friend who was going to L'Arche showed me a list of the French *foyers*, indicating one she thought was in the South. They replied, almost by return, saying I could come as soon as I liked – they needed a cook. The letter bore the post-mark 'La Somme'!

So, one cold October evening in 1980, I arrived, with limited cooking skills and 'A'-level French, at the L'Arche community in the Somme which was to be home for the next year. There were 12 residents at the *foyer*: eight of 'them', including the famous co-founder of L'Arche, Raphaël, and four assistants. I knew virtually nothing of Jean Vanier nor of L'Arche's spirituality except that the idea was to get away from the 'us' and 'them' distinction.

It was a warm but pretty chaotic welcome and I soon realized that my 'A'-level French was woefully inadequate. So did they. They were all very patient and took '*la jeune Anglaise*' (who managed nevertheless to communicate that she was '*Galloise*') under their wings. This was my first experience of a 'L'Arche' reversal. *I* was the one who was 'poor' and this became a great advantage in building relationships and being accepted. My first assumption of 'helping them' had been swept aside. As the year progressed (and my French with it) they showed me other areas of my poverty. People with learning difficulties are far from saints and can often be, as Jean Vanier himself admits, impossible. You learn you have less patience than you thought; you are horrified that you can have such feelings of anger and rage even, at these – and the word was still used in those days – 'handicapped' people. So they showed me my own 'handi-caps', my need for forgiveness and acceptance: another L'Arche reversal.

But they also showed me riches, sides of myself of which I was barely aware or had lost sight of in an intense academic environment. An Oxford degree cut no ice with them but presence did, kindness did. They let me know I was OK to be around for no other reason than that of being myself. That is enormously liberating. And something to celebrate. It was at L'Arche that I learned how to celebrate: birthdays, name-days, arrivals, anniversaries, departures and the feasts of the Church. And the core of each celebration was the celebration of the mystery of each person and the gift of life. Their ability to celebrate in the midst of some pretty awful personal histories and circumstances was infectious and gave me a sense of admiration for their courage and a certain perspective on my own 'problems'. I re-learned how to play. Our village was more of a hamlet where you had to make your own recreation (music, cycling, walking, crafts) and where church and postbox were the only amenities. Not that there was too much leisure time, for the ordinary things of life, washing, chores, shopping, take so much longer in the L'Arche world, especially when you try to live them the L'Arche way, that is, by letting people do as much as they can themselves even when it would be ten times quicker to do it yourself.

I left the following summer with a deeper faith in God and humanity; more self-knowledge and self-acceptance; my original preference for 'being' over 'doing' restored; pretty fluent French and an unquantifiable degree in 'body language'; a repertoire of French dishes with which to entertain for years ahead, an expanded waistline and many friends. Although I wasn't aware of it at the time, I feel sure that the seeds of my conversion to Roman Catholicism (six years later) and my vocation as a Benedictine (nine years later) were sown in that formative experience at L'Arche. (Something like 25 vocations to the priesthood or religious

59

life have emerged from that one small *foyer* in the past 20-odd years.) Maybe this is connected with the depth of self-knowledge which the L'Arche environment fosters. It is a privileged place of 'listening' to the heart – the level from which most of those with learning difficulties seem to operate and be 'experts' in. So, yes, my friend was right: 'community' was very important to me.

ENCOUNTERS WITH THE RULE OF ST BENEDICT

The would-be monk and I never discussed the Catholic faith per se and there was certainly no attempt to convert me. He did, however, present me with a copy of *The Rule of St Benedict* which I read and re-read. This was my first encounter with *The Rule* which was to shape and guide my journey to God as it has those of countless others both inside and outside monasteries these past 1,500 years. What struck me most about *The Rule*, initially, was its accessibility and humanity, the way it makes provision for the monks' oversleeping, for example, and although I didn't make the connection at the time, it was those same qualities of openness and humanity which had attracted me to Dom Leo, who was, therefore, I suppose, more really my first encounter with Benedict's *Rule*. Those who live by *The Rule* are formed by it, come to incarnate its values and help keep it a living text rather than an ancient document. It is no coincidence that many communities choose to situate the compulsory daily reading of *The Rule* in the context of a shared meal where the text 'feeds' the listeners' hearts as surely as their bodies are physically sustained by the food.

Since then, and especially in my work of helping to induct newcomers to monastic life, I have come to appreciate Benedict's *Rule* as one of the great formative texts of Western civilization. The Chief Rabbi, Jonathan Sacks, has suggested[3] that greatness can be measured in terms of that towards which one effaces oneself. I think something similar may be said of *The Rule* which constantly points the reader beyond itself, to Scripture – primarily to the Gospel, but also to the early Christian and monastic writers and even to the Eastern Rule(s) of St Basil. In this way it seems to incarnate the humility it seeks to teach. *The Rule* guides those who follow it, not so much as a blueprint but more as a road map or, better still, a compass which gives a constant Godward orientation to the journey, no matter how poorly marked the way ahead.

> When we are ready to make a new beginning ... we are given subtle hints, inner signals that alert us to the proximity of new beginnings. We get faint intimations; we hear a subtle new theme in the music; we ... catch a strange new fragrance on the breeze, and we begin to discern the shape of the next step.[4]

St Benedict haunted me that summer: conversations with the most unlikely people would turn to him and books about him seemed to leap off bookshelves into my hands. To cap it all, when staying with a friend in Norwich, I had to face a daily gauntlet run through the St Benedict district of the city, where his name embellishes all kinds of establishments from dry-cleaners to off-licences.

That same summer (1986), I was given a *Book of Common Prayer* and started to read the *Te Deum* and the *Venite* each day (more incipient Benedictinism). A third person provided a piece of knotted string and introduced me to the Jesus Prayer. I wouldn't have accepted a rosary then, still being somewhat anti-Catholic, but a knotted string was alright. God works as he can and was certainly laying many foundation stones without my being in the least aware of them.

That autumn of 1986 the young man from the car-park entered the monastery. And it was in the gap left by his absence that I decided to occupy myself with the stained-glass trail that Saturday ... I think this is where we came in.

GO WEST!

I never wanted to be a nun – I had a distinct antipathy towards them, and would run away or hide in my mother's skirts whenever a habited figure crossed our path in the streets, which was not infrequently in the early 1960s. My desire had always been to teach, to be married and to have six children (there were five children in our family and it was an awkward number for slicing up cakes). It is hardly surprising then, that on sensing so strong a call to forsake all that for the life of an enclosed nun, my immediate reaction should have been one of panic rather than *fiat*. Still, it wasn't a 'no' and at some deep, intangible level there was even a kind of attraction. It came as a relief, even so, to learn that one could not enter religious life until one had spent at least two years as a Roman Catholic. I tried to get back to 'normal' life. But while my job in a young and dynamic geography department of a large urban comprehensive school continued to be both challenging and rewarding, the inner ache would not go away. It was as if an invisible film had formed between myself and the rest of life so that I could not enter fully into anything.

Dom Leo was marvellously directive: his summary advice was that I needed to distance myself from the situation. 'Go to the States', he said, 'get yourself on some kind of course'. The postgraduate course for experienced teachers which was being piloted at Harvard the following year seemed ideal and, by some quirk of providence, a couple of scholarships of the highly specific kind – 'teachers from Swansea who wish to further their studies in the States' sort of thing – were available and so the whole enterprise became financially viable. Divine Providence was to guide that whole year (1988–89) in a remarkable way. One example will have to stand for the rest.

Owing to one of those 'Catch 22' visa problems where you need proof of funding to secure a visa, and a visa to secure the funding and college placement, there was some delay in getting all the necessary documentation, and so I arrived in Boston just before the Fall semester when most student accommodation had already been snapped up. All the more surprising, then, to find an apartment-share in a central location and at a reasonable cost, but it soon became apparent why this one had been avoided by others as the contract stipulated all kinds of rather bizarre *obligata*, including the expectation that the tenant would be quiet and provide a vacuum cleaner (surely mutually exclusive demands). My budget, even with the scholarships and the library job I'd secured, was still pretty tight and did not stretch to buying luxuries like vacuum cleaners and so it was suggested that I should try that great American phenomenon: the yard sale. I set out one Saturday morning with just two items on my shopping list: a vacuum cleaner and a table lamp for my otherwise sparsely furnished room. They were clearing up when I arrived (the Americans are usually 'up and doing' long before their transatlantic cousins). 'Too bad you missed the sale' said one of the cashiers. 'Why don't you take a look at what's left?' 'Sure' I replied, stepping into the adjoining room where there were precisely two items: a table lamp (minus shade) and a vacuum cleaner (possibly Hoover's prototype). To my 'just what I wanted' the young chap nodded somewhat incredulously and let me take the goods for nothing!

This was just the prelude to God's gifts during that graced year. He added friends, a vibrant parish community, opportunities for travel, the chance to get to know many of Boston's street people, as well as the thrill of the Harvard course, my ostensible reason for being there. He even provided for my more covert motivation: the eight o'clock Mass congregation included an architect of about my own age who was taking a year out to discern a possible future with the Jesuits. Many were the coffees shared as we tried to make sense of this mysterious thing called 'vocation'.

Amid all these riches, the inner pull of Stanbrook persisted and grew even stronger. The fact that I was enjoying life and could see all sorts of alternative futures opening up served to reassure me that I wasn't running away from life but had real choices. This, in turn, seemed to make opting for Stanbrook more of a free decision. And so, with great peace and some ceremony, I wrote to the abbess from the Weidener Library in Harvard in the presence of a Gutenberg Bible. On the face of it my request was to spend three weeks inside the monastic enclosure in order to discern the next step. But in my heart it was tantamount to entering for life.

THREE WEEKS 'INSIDE'

As it turned out, the three weeks 'inside' proved quite a tussle – perhaps the wrench of leaving the States was still too fresh for me to enter fully into the next new experience. On one level, I felt completely at home: the rhythm of the monastic offices, the balance of the day between prayer and work resonated with something deep within me. But it seemed a tune well beyond my range. The Gospel on the first day of my stay was: 'he who loves his life loses it; he who hates his life in this world will keep it for eternal life' (Jn

12.25). That was the problem – I loved my life too much, just as it was, and didn't want to lose it. The old questions and doubts re-emerged: wouldn't it be more useful to teach in an inner-city school? Wasn't I made for marriage? How could I ever cope with enclosure? And then there was the nagging suspicion that I wasn't good enough for this life where everyone seemed so saintly. Last, but not least, there was the impossibility of living so far from the sea. At the end of the three weeks I coolly thanked the abbess and informed her that I felt sure God was calling me back to teaching. Mother Abbess replied, probably not without irony which was lost on me at the time, that she was glad things had become so clear, and promised to pray for me.

Stanbrook prayers can be pretty powerful, I was to discover shortly, but my more immediate discovery, on leaving the abbey, was a sickening sense of loss, like a bereavement. It took some plain talking from Dom Leo to get things in focus. 'So, you never felt more at home; the balance and rhythm of the day suited you; you liked almost everything about the place but you don't think God is calling you there? And now you feel desolate. Is that it?' It did sound less than logical. We agreed that I should write and ask for more time to consider the decision. The peace felt on posting the letter was beyond telling and such a contrast to the disturbed state experienced after the previous decision that it was fairly easy, with the help of a guide, to see from where the two sensations were coming. Almost exactly a year later, on 23 September 1990, I entered Stanbrook, wearing a riotously colourful pair of the half-masted trousers that were in vogue at the time, a shocking pink T-shirt and long dangling earrings, all of which prompted at least one of the sisters to predict a rapid exit. I also had – I hope less evidently – a lingering hangover from my last night out in the world.

DARKNESS AND LIGHT

The date of entrance happened to coincide with the celebration of the Feast of the Conception of John the Baptist in the Eastern Church, and though not chosen for that, it became significant for me in those darkening days of autumn and winter when, after the relief of arriving, the hiddenness of life in the novitiate began to strike home. Some lines I wrote about that time speak of more than the season:

> Autumn
> A time of transition
> as the leaves die.
> There is beauty in the
> leaving. Leaving a
> Sacred space for God.
> A time to consider the holly,
> – evergreen –
> His abiding presence
> through all transitions.

It *was* a kind of death leading to rebirth, a conception that would lead to new life as we moved towards the Feast of the Birth of John the Baptist the following summer. In the meantime, the dying feelings of darkness, loneliness, isolation and strangeness existed alongside a sense of being in exactly the right place and going through a necessary process.

At times, the tune becomes scrambled, degenerates into noise or becomes so faint that one thinks it has ceased altogether. I remember, one day during my early months in the monastery, trying to explain this to the novice mistress: 'It's as if I'm a piece of sculpture', I said, 'and huge chunks of me are falling to the ground.' She seemed quite pleased. While I'd expected a certain amount of rubbing off of awkward corners, nothing had prepared me for the wholesale demolition job the novitiate seemed to be. Never one to rush in with easy explanations, the novice mistress, who was unfailingly kind and supportive, usually left me to puzzle out these things alone.

The hardest thing was to see what seemed like the better parts of oneself – friendships, competencies, a certain healthy self-confidence that had taken years to build up – coming under the sculptor's hammer (though all would be given back later, hopefully freed from at least a few layers of ego). Newcomers to monastic life are generally not given jobs that demand a great deal of thought or responsibility, and this quite intentionally so as to allow the real work of the novitiate, the coming to birth of the true self, dependent as that is on the dismantling of the false or ego self, to at least begin. That is the theory. More than theory, that is the truth as taught by all the monastic teachers and spiritual writers through the ages, going right back to Christ himself: if anyone wants to be a follower of mine let him renounce himself, take up his cross and follow me; back to saving life by losing it.

At first, the lack of responsibility, the variation on a theme of washing up, came as something of a relief after the stress of teaching, but gradually I came to realize just how much of myself was defined by my job. This lack of self-realization through work, coupled with being distanced from loved ones, left a real void and sense of inner emptiness. Community support, which I'm sure was real enough, wasn't all that palpable since in those days (this has now changed) we operated a closed novitiate, that is, one where there was no contact permitted between novitiate members and community except at recreation on Sundays

67

and Holy days. Coming from a large and close family and having always been blessed with good friends, I found this isolation hard to bear, especially as my personality isn't all that outgoing. Without prayer it would have been unbearable, but I suppose that was the point. The novitiate experience is supposed to have something of the desert about it, is supposed to throw us back on God. The psalms took on a new and deeper meaning:

'It is your face, O Lord, that I seek,
hide not your face' (Psalm 26[27].8).

'O Lord, it is you who are my portion and cup;
it is you yourself who are my prize ...
You will show me the path of life,
the fullness of joy in your presence,
at your right hand happiness for ever'
(Psalm 15[16].5, 11).

Gradually, the daily round of communal prayer, the rhythm of manual labour interspersed with study and the deepening of one's knowledge of Christ in the Scriptures, began to bring a sense of peace. The joy of picking apples in the October sun, of following the subtle changes in light in the eastern rose window throughout the day, of feeling physically tired at night, are happy memories of this time. There was also satisfaction in learning new skills such as habit-making. (That I ever made friends with a sewing machine was convincing proof for the family of the authenticity of my vocation.) So, on late autumn afternoons in the sewing room, looking up from the black garments to see the sun's low rays ignite the last acacia leaves in the rockery, one could catch the tune again and sense oneself in the music.

WITHIN THESE WALLS: LIVING 'ENCLOSURE'

Often in life it seems the things we dread don't happen, or at least aren't as bad as we fear, while the real difficulties only emerge when we are in a particular situation and can hardly be anticipated. I suppose this has something to do with the level of unreality most of us live with a lot of the time. Before entering the monastery, I'd wondered how I'd cope with 'enclosure', that is, with the discipline of living within the confines of the abbey walls (for the sake of fostering prayer) except for 'necessary exits'. Although what qualifies as a 'necessary exit' has broadened considerably over the past 30 or so years to include, for example, study courses as well as medical attention, we do not normally visit family (except in the case of the grave illness or death of a parent) or go away on holiday. To my surprise, as one who had relished travel and visiting friends, this has never been a problem. (Not that it wasn't hard to miss the weddings of my brother and sister.) I've found what others, who have become less voluntarily housebound through illness, have no doubt discovered: that to get to know one small piece of God's earth very well is a blessing, and to be spared the often taxing choice of where next to go on holiday a kind of liberation. It's a question of depth of experience against that compulsive need to experience everything which can lead to superficiality: 'Promiscuity is not the seed-bed of love', as Dom Dominic Gaisford wrote memorably in his monastic journey in the original *Touch of God*.[5] He was speaking about celibacy, but enclosure, too, fosters a certain chastity of heart and a greater clarity of vision. To witness the seasons play out their annual symphony and to watch, at close range, those changes reflected in the myriad patterns of nature, is one of the unexpected pleasures of the enclosed life; and, as one becomes more attuned to the rhythms of the liturgical year, one begins to glimpse something of that wholeness of life which was probably more evident to our forebears who lived closer to the land. The spareness of a winter landscape matches the haunting, unaccompanied chants of Advent, for example, while the eruption of green and the procession of spring flowers from snowdrop, through daffodil to bluebell, chime in with the joyful alleluias of Easter when all Creation shouts with St Mary Magdalene, '*Surrexit Christus, spes mea*', 'Christ, my hope, is risen.'

So, for me, 'enclosure' is both an aid to, and a symbol of, a kind of simplification of my life, a practice which helps root me in the here and now and plugs me into an international, and through the communion of saints, extraterrestrial and eternal, network of communication. In other words, it has nothing to with being cut off from the world, and everything to do with making connections. Henri Nouwen, writing on the Parable of the Prodigal Son, speaks of the father's 'radical discipline'[6] of staying at home: not a bad definition of 'enclosure' and one we are all called to embrace at some stage in life as our sphere of physical activity shrinks and we appear to move in ever-diminishing circles. By accepting and even choosing those things which we can't change and seem to limit us, it becomes possible to break through into a new dimension. For the Welsh poet, Waldo Williams, life is 'Finding a spacious hall between narrow walls'[7]; words that can be applied to the discovery of freedom in any situation that threatens to hem us in.

'TO SING IS TO PRAY TWICE'

And then there was singing. I have often wondered what is meant by the words, usually attributed to St Augustine, 'to sing well is to pray twice', and am still not sure, but few things have brought me to my knees in a state of utter helplessness as singing has. To say that this came as a surprise to one from Wales, the land of song, is an understatement. Perhaps that was the problem. Having more or less always sung in choirs, I wasn't expecting to have to work at it. But a monastic choir is completely different, comprising the whole community, not just the singers. Put bluntly: they found me arrogant and I found them flat. No doubt I *was* arrogant, but deliberately to sing what sounded below the note was for me like lying, and so not something easy to do given my home background where to tell the truth had been drummed into us as children. Singing, even solo singing, is, I believe, an intensely corporate activity (was that what St Augustine was getting at? One sings oneself and in the body?), so my attitude set me off, not on the wrong note (that was them) but definitely on the wrong foot for someone starting out on the path of humility. I found, not surprisingly, by my strident insistence on singing the 'right' note, that I'd lost the goodwill of the choir and that, without their support, I couldn't sing freely. A divinely sent fail-safe mechanism, perhaps? It was as if all one's worst traits of self-righteousness and self-sufficiency came to the fore in this holy and, oh so public, forum. Learning to sing with the body of the monastic choir has been for me a kind of microcosm of all the challenges of living in community: to listen, to contribute one's gifts and talents but not to dominate, to appreciate and accept the gifts, talents and limitations of others and oneself, and sometimes even to sing what may seem to one's own ear the wrong note for the sake of a deeper harmony.

This is not the place to embark on an exposition of the significance of the Divine Office, so central to Benedictines, but as well as telling us to 'prefer nothing to Christ', St Benedict also says we should 'put nothing before the Work of God', the Divine Office. Increasingly, I have come to see these as one: Christ, as head of his body, the Church, is the one singing the psalms, and in him all dissonance is taken up and transformed – not without tears – into *a tune beyond us*. And there are moments of supreme joy in choir, moments that seem to touch heaven, where 'you are the music while the music lasts'.[8] In between the agony and the ecstasy are many steady, unspectacular offices, a kind of heartbeat, as a guest listening to our choir once described it. This heartbeat goes on continually whether there are guests or not. Early on in the monastery, it struck me that the phrase sung at Compline, 'May the Lord Almighty grant us a quiet night and a perfect end', was not about a group of women asking for a good night's sleep for themselves but was rather Christ's prayer to the Father for the whole world, a prayer we are privileged to share.

FALLING AND RISING

As the end of the novitiate years drew near, life seemed bearable. I had, by then, been given responsibility for the habit-making department, a job I enjoyed for its creativity and the opportunities it offered to establish a personal link with each sister. But there was still a sense of isolation and of not yet being fully at home or myself. Walks and cycle rides in the enclosure were a source of strength and consolation and provided the necessary space to put things in perspective. On one such walk, in the winter of 1995, I recall thinking, 'as long as I can get outside like this, I can cope.' These were to be famous last words ...

Laetare Sunday, the day we celebrate Mother Abbess' Feast-Day, was particularly busy for me that year. Traditionally, the novitiate decorates the refectory on a theme, and this particular year, under my direction, we were to illustrate the six days of Creation from the book of

Genesis; an ambitious project, but I had it all worked out. A slight twinge of awareness impinged on my conscience, as we put up the displays, that perhaps I had it worked out all *too* well, that perhaps a spot more interaction with the other members of the novitiate may not have gone amiss. But it was too late for conversion that year: the design was a success and enjoyed by the community.

The highlight of the celebration came on the Sunday afternoon when some of us were to perform an adaptation of the dying swan sequence from Swan Lake. A sister who had formerly been a professional ballerina took the lead role and had also trained, over a period of some weeks, several of us 'cygnets' as the *corps de ballet*. Seconds into the dance, I felt what seemed like a bullet wound in my left calf. The pain was excruciating and the leg trailed limp, as this cygnet struggled to keep up with the others. The audience clearly thought this was all part of the act for they laughed appreciatively. Only when the applause died away, and I was left as a heap on the floor, did they realize that something was wrong. It took two sisters and a wheelchair to get the invalid to her cell and it would be a whole year before she recovered fully from what turned out to be a ruptured Achilles tendon. Those walks and cycle rides came to an abrupt end.

God is indeed that 'jealous God who tolerates no rivals' spoken of in the anonymous mediaeval treatise on prayer, *The Cloud of Unknowing* (Ch. 2). This is not to suggest for an instant that I think God was punishing my innocent walks; rather, it seems to me that he showed me, via the accident, things I was clinging to in a possessive way. God wants us for himself and he wants us to rely wholly on him. It was the lesson Moses and the Israelites had to learn as they wandered in the wilderness for 40 years en route to the Promised Land, and one I find that I'm constantly having to relearn on the journey through life. Those idols we are warned against at the end of the First Letter of St John needn't be as obviously idolatrous as a golden calf; they can be as subtle as wanting to be in control or as innocuous as a walk in the grounds.

The time of enforced immobility, waiting for the tendon to mend, gave me a lot of time to reflect and so was the ideal preparation for Solemn Profession (of vows), as once again I was forced back on prayer. Often, when we look back, we can perceive challenging events as something positive, but even at the time this accident struck me as providential. Something else, something more interior, seemed to have 'snapped' and I felt a kind of relief and freedom and a renewed sense of God's closeness and care. My affliction turned out to be far more of a bridge than a barrier as community members went out of their way to help and, for once, I was powerless to refuse. Being on the receiving end of so much kindness and acceptance recalled the time at L'Arche and I think helped me to a deeper level of acceptance of myself and others. A particular blessing of life on the infirmary wing was the company of the more elderly nuns whose patience and humour proved a powerful mixture.

Best of all was the delight of gradually re-finding all those things that had been lost during the months of convalescence: the larch in the far field, the wildlife at the pond, the full round of services in church. It was like a re-entry where everything was given back imbued with a new shininess. It was a resurrection as surely as entering the monastery and all that had ensued was a kind of death. It was a palpable experience of living the Paschal Mystery and one that has been repeated, if not always as dramatically, many times since. Resurrection is the keynote of the Christian life.

The unfinished tasks we have tried to do, the dreams and hopes and aspirations after which we have striven, the relationships we have vainly sought to perfect and complete, the experiences which have lifted us and laid us low, moulded us and made us – all these will not be lost or left behind, but will be the notes by which we render harmony to the music of the City of God. By the Resurrection of Jesus Christ we know that all that is of good or can be made so will never perish, but will be exalted to the heavenly places and clothed with the divine power, if only it be freely surrendered by us to that death which is the boundary line of our present existence.[9]

'A TUNE BEYOND US, YET OURSELVES'

This theme tune has run right through my monastic life to date and I suspect will run and run, for it is the tune of our Benedictine vows of obedience, *conversatio* (or conversion of life by the monastic way) and stability, vows which are themselves rooted in Christ's own obedience to the Father, his journey from this world to the next, in the lee of which the Christian follows and is taken up. When one of our senior nuns learned I was to be clothed in the habit during the Easter Octave she sent a warm note of congratulation and urged me to try to take my vows in the Octave too. These things are quite beyond a novice's control, of course, but through God's Providence, so it turned out that all my key dates have been in the Easter Octave, in the wake of the Lord's Resurrection. While each person's significant dates are just that, for me, the need to be pulled along in the slipstream of the resurrected and ascending Christ is essential. Only in his strength can one go on responding to the call – for a vocation is for life, not just for Christmas – to move out of oneself, out of all that's familiar, into the spaciousness of God. The unfamiliar always seems beyond me, whether it's a case of a new chant to be learned or a new job to be tackled, a blank page to be filled with text or the more intimate call to a deepening of prayer. But the leap *is* made with the Lord's help and, once there, one feels held even if it can take longer to feel at home. In essence, I suppose what I'm learning is that this repeating motif of movement into stability and of dynamism in stability, so central to the Benedictine *Rule*, is nothing less than our journey into the life of the Trinity. A tune completely beyond us, yet one, by God's gift, we are invited to sing.

Bring us, O Lord God, at our last awakening, into the house and gate of heaven, to enter into that gate, and to dwell in that house where there shall be no cloud nor sun, no darkness nor dazzling, but one equal light; no noise nor silence, but one equal music; no fears nor hopes, but one equal possession; no foes nor friends, but an equal communion and identity; no ends nor beginnings, but one equal eternity in the habitation of thy glory and dominion, world without end. Amen.

(John Donne, Sermon XV)

NOTES

1. W. Stevens (1954), 'The Man with the Blue Guitar', *The Collected Poems of Wallace Stevens*. New York: Knopf; London: Faber and Faber, p. 165.
2. T. Radcliffe (2001), *I Call You Friends*. London: Continuum, pp. 100–101.
3. Sacks, J., 'Endangered virtues 3: humility', *The Tablet*, 1 April 2000, p. 451.

4. W. Bridges, reprinted in J. Fowler, *Faith Development & Pastoral Care*, Fortress Press.

5. M. Boulding (ed.) (1982), *A Touch of God*. London: SPCK, p. 167.

6. H. J. M. Nouwen (1992), *The Return of the Prodigal Son*. London: Darton, Longman & Todd, p. 124.

7. W. Williams (1956), *Dail Pren*. Aberystwyth. The translation is my own.

8. T. S. Eliot (1959), The Dry Salvages, *Four Quartets*. London: Faber and Faber, p. 44, l. 211.

9. N. Clark (1967), *Interpreting the Resurrection*. London: SCM Press, pp. 114–15.

4

The Most Unexpected Places

Martin McGee

Growing up in Newport, County Mayo in the West of Ireland in the 1950–60s was to absorb faith as easily as the fields absorbed the plentiful showers of rain. Faith was a natural part of existence and Catholicism was practised by almost 100 per cent of the farming community. My mother was a woman of strong faith though by no means uncritical of the clergy who reigned unchallenged. I absorbed this faith in the same way that I learnt to speak English, to walk and to run. It was part of learning to mature and to discover the secrets of existence. I remember as a young child telling people that I would become a priest when I grew up and that my mother would come to live with me in the presbytery. However, I quickly ceased to speak of this idea as I didn't want to become its hostage.

Who could ever have imagined that almost a half-century later I would, as a monk and priest of Worth Abbey, look out of an aeroplane window on Thursday, 7 April 2005 and, with growing excitement, see the Algerian coastline for the first time just as a brutal civil war was petering out. On my return to Worth I wrote to Mgr Henri Teissier, Archbishop of Algiers, to thank him for *la plus belle semaine de ma vie* – the best week of my life. How could that be, you may ask? Was this sentence an example of my Celtic tendency to exaggerate? I am not sure that a clear answer can be given. As a Francophile, the love-hate relationship of the French people with Algeria had drawn me to that country. Above all, however, I had been drawn there by the 19 Christian martyrs who had offered their lives (1994–96) out of love for a Muslim people. In a sense I was on a pilgrimage to discover the source of this love which ultimately flows from Jesus' love for us, a love which impelled him freely to offer his life on our behalf. So perhaps here was to be found the deepest motivation for my strange interest and journey, and also my motivation for becoming a monk.

ONE PERSON WHO IS CHRIST-LIKE

At the age of 13 in 1964 I set out for the diocesan boarding school. This was an unusual school in that it was the only secondary school in Ireland where, for four of my five years there, all members of the teaching staff were priests. It was an institution which was run on strict disciplinary lines with very little scope for individuality. The regime was semi-monastic with three compulsory church services a day. Another demanding aspect of life was the poor quality of the food. In fact I remember reading recently an account of life in a Japanese prisoner-of-war camp for civilians and it struck me that their allocation of food was scarcely worse than what we had on offer in those Lenten times. The daily round of church and prayer no doubt left its indelible mark but what strikes me now is how ritualized and impersonal it all was. The prayers were all standardized. We didn't have spontaneous intercessions nor did we pray for other members of the College at any of the services, nor was it the custom to ask any of the priests to pray for an intention.

Despite the rather dismal picture which I have painted above, there were compensating factors. We had a strong sense of the transcendent and the holy and a strong sense of right and wrong. And, above all, several of the priests had attractive personalities and lived out the Christian life in a humane manner. They showed us the attractiveness of the Gospel message and made Christianity credible. After all, for the Gospels to come alive all that is required is that there be one person who is Christ-like. And I was fortunate enough to meet among the priests at least four or five such people who in one way or another by their lives showed me aspects of Christ's teaching being put into practice. This effort to live out the Gospel message of fraternal love takes Christianity out of the realm of an antiquated ideology and into the realm of a life-giving way.

The two people who most exemplified Gospel living for me were my mother and one of the priests in the College, Fr Enda Lyons. My mother took her religious practice seriously; it was the centre of her life. However, lots of people in those days were scrupulous about obeying the laws of the Church. What made my mother's practice of her religion attractive were her prayer life, unselfish devotion to her family and openness to those in need. She didn't preach about Christianity but tried to live it in the simple events of everyday life. For example, I remember at the age of about 10 taking a Christmas cake made by my mother to an elderly neighbour living on his own. Also every time I returned from boarding school I would be given the job of sending off money to support various missionary priests, though as a family we could ill afford to part with these donations. Likewise, when the itinerants, or travellers, would visit, my mother always gave them some food and money. Indeed one of these travelling women took the trouble to attend my mother's funeral. I now realize that my mother had sensed the great hardship and suffering which these people had to endure in those days. Fr Lyons' impact was of a different kind. His willingness to listen to the pain of others and his respect for difference were striking, as was his personal integrity. It was a great blessing and relief to be able to pour out my heart to him at the age of 17 in my penultimate year at secondary school. Both my mother and Fr Enda showed me, each in a different way, that the Gospel was indeed Good News.

Another key experience in my religious awakening also took place at this time: my 'conversion' experience, if it's not too grandiose a word. As a primary school boy I had often heard the word 'charity' being mentioned and understood it to mean the act of giving money to the poor. One Sunday morning in my first year at boarding school I heard a homily which explained St Paul's understanding of charity as patience, kindness and so on, a way of living which tried to put other people first in the nitty-gritty of daily life. My eyes were opened and I understood for the first time that this was what it meant to be a Christian. And I was given the grace to put some of my new insights into practice. So when, for example, I returned home for the holidays, I tried to be more attentive to my mother and when asked to run to the shops, I would do so without complaining. (I hope my memory is not playing tricks on me!) I had made an important breakthrough in realizing that Christianity is above all a way of life. It is in trying to live this Gospel way of life that we gradually penetrate more and more into the mysteries of the faith. St Augustine sums up this insight beautifully in the phrase, 'For us, to live is to love.' And this is why I have never been tempted to abandon the practice of the Christian faith because I know that love is at the heart of Christianity and that it is love which gives life its savour and fruitfulness.

THE FREEDOM OF UNIVERSITY

After the austere regime of boarding school, University College, Galway, in October 1969 was like entering a land of plenty. I was free to be myself and rejoiced in the sense of freedom and intellectual ferment to be found on the campus. My main subjects were Philosophy and French, both of which I loved. From a very early age I had wanted to speak French and found the atmosphere of things French intoxicating. Reading *Vol de Nuit* by Antoine de Saint-Exupéry in my first year was like entering an exotic garden whose scents and flowers entranced me, though I was unable to name many of them. At secondary school I had learnt to read and write French but the language wasn't spoken at all in the classroom.

At the end of my first year at university I spent three months in France doing voluntary work for the *Petits Frères des Pauvres*, a charitable organization which provides support for elderly people in Paris and some of the other major cities. I went to work in their holiday châteaux for two months and then spent a month in Paris visiting the elderly in their tiny apartments, often on the sixth floor without access to a lift. I was to spend several summers working as a volunteer with the *Petits Frères*. This was an ideal way to remedy my complete lack of spoken French and to begin to absorb the French way of doing things. Visiting the elderly in their homes and listening to their stories was a great privilege and I always felt very close to God while working with them. Without being aware of it consciously, I was meeting the Lord in these lonely and impoverished old ladies. While in Paris I also, by some sort of homing instinct, discovered the Lord's presence in the wonderful Sunday liturgies at some of the churches in the Latin Quarter. Saint-Germain-des-Prés, a former Benedictine Abbey of the St

Maur Congregation, was my favourite church but I also attended Mass in Saint-Sulpice and Saint-Séverin. After the rather mechanical celebration of the Sunday Mass which I had been used to in Ireland, the dignity of the celebration and the fervour and commitment of the congregation as well as the high standard of preaching and singing were very inspiring.

University was a time of intellectual excitement and a growing self-confidence after the battering which my fragile sense of self had suffered at boarding school. I was always more self-confident in an academic setting than in a social one. For example, even at secondary school I would very willingly express my views in front of the class but this confidence didn't carry over into life outside the classroom. At university there was the freedom to find one's own persona without the critical appraisal of an adolescent group with its inevitable pressures to conform. There was only one Catholic chaplain for about 2,500 students and I only spoke to him on one or two occasions. I attended Mass on Sundays at a nearby Jesuit church. At the time there was an active evangelical group on the campus, which I think was part of the Campus Crusade for Christ group, with whom I had some wary contact. It was strange and unfamiliar to hear the evangelical emphasis on Scripture and to listen to their conversion testimonies. I remember one of the leaders of the group giving me a paper to read explaining why the Catholic teaching of the Real Presence of Christ in the Eucharist was unbiblical. I never read it as I feared that it might undermine my faith. Despite so hesitant a start, this was probably my first real encounter with another tradition and helped to foster my interest in ecumenism. I've always felt an attraction to those who are different, as I sense that they can teach me new ways of looking at life and enrich me by so doing. This evangelical group put the spotlight on Christ rather than on the institutional Church, a welcome adjustment to the religion of my youth.

THREE MONASTIC EXPERIENCES: TAIZÉ, MELLIFONT AND GLENSTAL

After my degree I spent a further year acquiring a teacher training qualification and then a year in Bordeaux as an English language assistant at the Lycée Michel Montaigne. On my return to Ireland I took up my first full-time teaching job in Bush, County Louth and after one year I moved into the Christian Brothers' School in nearby Dundalk. This was a school where I felt at home from day one. There was a full range of academic ability among the students and most of them were keen to learn. It was while here that I discovered the existence of Taizé in France and most summers I would spend a week there. I was very struck by the Bible study groups where the Word of God seemed so alive and active. The Brothers could speak about the Bible passages as if they had been written yesterday and like the disciples on the road to Emmaus my heart was burning within me as I listened to them. Without my experience of going to Taizé I think it would have taken me much longer to discover a monastic vocation.

The second monastic experience which I had at this time of my life was Cistercian. There was a Cistercian monastery, Mellifont Abbey, about 15 miles from Dundalk. Early on in my time at the Christian Brothers' School I was asked to accompany one of the history teachers on a class outing. As part of the day we called in to Mellifont Abbey to visit the shop and maze. The teacher told me that it was possible to go to the Abbey for a retreat. I knew nothing about monastic life apart from having read Thomas Merton's

84

autobiography, *The Seven Storey Mountain*, the story of how he came to join the Trappist monastery of Gethsemani in America. The idea of spending a weekend at the monastery appealed to me. On my arrival I was pleasantly surprised when the guest master carried my bag up to my room. Fr Finnian, later Abbot Finnian, was a humble and impressive man, very different from some of the overbearing parish clergy of the time. I got into the habit of visiting Mellifont for a weekend at the start of each school year in September. My two days there would fill me with a sense of peace which kept me going for months. However, I never considered joining the community as their very enclosed and austere way of life didn't appeal to me. I didn't want to lose contact with people. In addition, their main source of work and income was farming which didn't appeal to me either. Although I had been brought up on a farm, unlike my three brothers, I had no aptitude for farming and heartily disliked almost everything to do with it.

My first contact with the Benedictines came about as a result of watching a television programme in 1980 celebrating the 1,500[th] anniversary of the birth of St Benedict. Two monks from Glenstal Abbey and a Cistercian monk from Mount St Joseph's Abbey, Roscrea, were interviewed about monastic life. I was very taken by the fact that they had no party line and clearly expressed their own point of view. They all had attractive personalities and lively minds and what they had to say was stimulating. As a result of this programme, I made my first visit to Glenstal Abbey in County Limerick. I made several subsequent visits and, at the suggestion of the guest master, Br Michael, began to consider seriously the question of a monastic vocation to Glenstal.

Joining a monastery is in many ways like getting married. Each Benedictine monastery has its own lived interpretation of the *Rule of St Benedict* and its own unique personality. So someone who feels called to the monastic way of life has to discern which monastic community suits them, just as someone attracted to the married way of life has to find the right person to whom they can commit themselves for life. The vow of stability commits a monk or nun to live with the same group of people for life. Finding the right monastery is about finding a community where you feel at home, where you can grow spiritually and as a person despite, or even on account of, the inevitable ups and downs of any living relationship. To find out if Glenstal would suit me and to enable the community to begin its own appraisal of my suitability to their way of life, I stayed for one month in the Abbey Guesthouse. Although the giftedness of the monks and the beauty of the surroundings strongly attracted me, I sensed that there was something in the air which didn't suit me; a certain tension in the community, a result, I imagine, of having so many creative people living under the same roof. In addition, I was worried about joining a community which appeared, at least to an outsider, to have very little outreach to the marginalized. I had too many reservations, all of which suggested that I would be unlikely to persevere if a request to join the novitiate were granted. I decided, wisely I think, not to pursue the relationship any further.

CHOOSING LIFE

Having decided not to apply to Glenstal, that same day I applied for a year's sabbatical from teaching to pursue an MA course in Guidance & Counselling at Durham University. As the year at Durham progressed, I still felt an attraction to the monastic way of life and what I had read about Worth Abbey suggested that it would suit me. It had a Lay Community and a mission in Peru, both of which made me think that I would find an outward-looking and open community. The only problem was my own inability to know if I really had a monastic vocation. It had taken me five years to discover that Glenstal was not for me. I was a ditherer! While living in Dundalk I was hesitant to put down roots by buying a house as I sensed that I would be moving on at some stage. I had several friends in Dundalk – male and female – but had no really close attachments. I felt an emptiness in my life and sensed that if I didn't find something deeper, spiritually I would slowly die. A point had been reached where, in the words of the book of Deuteronomy, I had to choose between life and death. But even so I was still quite unsure about what that choice should be. I lacked a clear sense of where God was calling me, tied in no doubt to a lack of self-knowledge.

As the year at Durham progressed, I sensed that I would need to make up my mind about monastic life. If I returned to teaching in Ireland I knew that it would be very difficult to extricate myself and make a fresh start. Fortunately, I received some clear pointers as to which direction I should choose. One Sunday evening I decided to attend Evensong at a city church. To my surprise it wasn't Evensong but some type of prayer meeting. During the service I suddenly decided to open the Bible at random and see if it would cast any light on my predicament. This was something which I had never done before. The edition contained both the Old and New Testaments and I opened it at Psalm 110 (Vulgate numbering). I started to read and thought to myself, 'This has nothing to say to me. It makes no sense at all.' And then my eyes came to the words, 'You are a priest forever after the order of Melchizedek' (Ps. 110.4, RSV). I was stunned and from that moment onwards I knew that I should give monastic life a go. My dithering was over. Those words from Psalm 110, in a matter of seconds, had put paid to five years of uncertainty. As a young person I had decided that I wasn't really suited to the responsibilities of being a parish priest, nor did I admire the power which the priesthood wielded at that time in Ireland, a power which placed priests on a pedestal. Nor was I attracted to the often lonely existence of the typical parish priest. However, I hadn't ruled out the possibility of becoming a priest in a monastic setting where the regular round of prayer and community life would provide companionship and keep my feet firmly on the ground.

Shortly afterwards as I was passing the Student Union building in Durham I wandered in to find that a Christian Union meeting was taking place. There were some leaflets on a table in the foyer. One attracted my attention, a booklet by John White called *Guidance*. As there was no one around, I put 50p on the table and took the booklet. It appeared to have been written especially for me. All my doubts and worries about monastic life were addressed – issues of location and certainty. The takeaway message which I found gave me great reassurance. In answering God's call mathematical certainty is not available. However, we can trust him because God wants our happiness more than we want it ourselves. I've still got the booklet and the phrase isn't exactly as I remembered it but it goes as follows:

Take courage, then, when you have a tough decision to make. Someone who cares deeply for you already knows what he wants you to do. He takes delight in having fellowship with you and wants the very circumstances you face to draw you closer to him. (p. 19)

MONASTIC LIVING

With this new-found conviction that I should give monastic life a try, I visited Worth Abbey and applied to join the novitiate. The then abbot, Victor Farwell, advised me first to spend some time in the Worth Lay Community so that the Worth monastic community could get to know me better and vice versa. During my six months in the Lay Community I followed the monastic routine and attended office in the Abbey Church, a building designed by Francis Pollen and consecrated in 1975. This is not a typical monastic church with Gothic arches and stained-glass windows. Although built in a square shape, it appears from the inside to be circular on account of the layout of the pillars and of the conical roof, open at the top to let in the light. The floor slopes towards the altar which is dominated by a large crucifix hanging from the roof. The sandy coloured bricks and carpet and the bare walls all produce a feeling of calm and simplicity, an atmosphere of stillness and of prayer. This modern, spaciously designed building, capable of seating well over a thousand people, embodies the spirit of the *Rule of St Benedict* by being both welcoming and unpretentious. The Abbey Church is the powerhouse of everything that goes on at Worth, the meeting place with the Spirit who heals and leads us into a closer union with God and with each other. Strangely enough, after my stay in the Lay Community, I had no hesitation in asking to join. My experience at Evensong in Durham had given me a confidence and a sense of calling which remained with me throughout my time in the Lay Community and in the years leading up to Final Vows.

My first impressions of the Worth monks, which have remained unchanged, were of friendly, down-to-earth and outward-looking people. We started off as four novices but by mid-February there were only two of us left. I didn't find the novitiate easy. Thirty-six years old at the time of joining, I was used to an independent lifestyle and marked by the individualism of our Western culture. As monastic life is an intense form of community living, it requires a certain suppleness in relationships. My boarding school experience and family background (I was the youngest of six) were undoubtedly assets. However, the novitiate by definition involves absorbing a new lifestyle – a demanding rhythm of communal and personal prayer, having one's daily routine mapped out, asking permissions, being under the constant gaze of the community and at the beck and call of the novice master. In addition, there is the shock which nearly all mature novices experience when they are stripped of responsibility and of all the props which give them status and independence. All of this routine and rhythm are, of course, designed in St Benedict's words 'to amend faults and to safeguard love'(*RB*, Prologue, 47). Despite the many challenges of this new way of life and of living outside Ireland, I never seriously doubted that I was in the right place. With hindsight, I see that my perseverance was a gift from God, the result of grace.

An essential of monastic living is reflective reading. When I entered the monastery we did a half-hour of spiritual reading every day. This involved reading a book on the spiritual life – it could be anything from Carlo Caretto's *Letters from the Desert* to *The Cloud of Unknowing*. I was always an avid reader and found this stimulating. However, in the early 1990s a change occurred when the practice of *lectio divina* was introduced at Worth. This is different from spiritual reading in that, firstly, Scripture is the primary text for *lectio*, and secondly, this is a form of reading which aims at allowing the text to be chewed over slowly so that it interacts with our daily life, leading us to prayer and conversion. This approach is more demanding than spiritual reading as it requires us to be more attentive and present to what we're reading and it also challenges us to be willing to be changed and converted, something which we don't always desire. The purpose of *lectio divina* is, to borrow a phrase from St Paul, to put on the mind of Christ (cf. 1 Cor. 2.16). The discovery of this ancient monastic practice has been a great blessing.

The third constant of monastic life, in addition to prayer and community life, is work. One of the things which attracted me to join Worth was our mission in Peru with its commitment to the developing world. Just before my Final Profession, to my disappointment, we closed down our house in Peru on account of the difficult political situation there but more especially on account of a lack of monk-power to sustain a viable community in Lima. (Worth still has one monk who is engaged full time in running Outreach Peru, an organization which supports charity and development projects.) My first job was teaching Religious Studies and some French in our school. In addition, I had some pastoral and chaplaincy duties. Five years ago I was appointed as full-time School Chaplain. As well as listening to the stories of individual students, helping them to produce a twice-yearly magazine, *Identity*, is probably one of the most worthwhile and enjoyable aspects of my chaplaincy involvement. This magazine tries to make the Benedictine ethos of the school more explicit and encourages students, staff and parents to reflect upon and write about what really matters to them. Through reflecting with honesty and compassion on their experience of life, many of the writers begin to discover God's presence at work even in experiences like death and divorce, events which at first sight promise nothing but pain and sorrow. The honesty of the Worth students, their friendliness and *joie de vivre*, their sense of God's presence; all of these provide a refreshing antidote to the jaded quality of much of modern life, a spirit of joy for which I am thankful.

A GROWING FASCINATION WITH ALGERIA

I have just mentioned the attraction which Peru exerted on me. The missionary instinct has always been part of the English Benedictine Congregation since its re-foundation on the Continent in the seventeenth century. In a rather unexpected way my missionary instinct has found in recent years an outlet through contact with the Algerian Church. The kidnapping of the seven Trappist monks of Tibhirine, a monastery located about 60 miles south of Algiers, in March 1996 by the GIA, an Islamic armed group, made media headlines throughout the world. Strangely enough, I can't recall following the story. In fact the plight of the Christian remnant in Algeria only gradually gripped my imagination, and the person responsible for this was Mgr Henri Teissier, Archbishop of Algiers. On 12 January 1997 *The Tablet* carried an interview with Mgr Teissier which deeply impressed me. I sensed something of his love for the Algerian people and his conviction that the Gospel was truly Good News, something of ultimate importance. The journalist wrote that he 'was moved by [his] visit to a priest of such dedication and fortitude'. Algeria at this time was caught up in a ruthless civil war between the Islamic fundamentalists who wished to impose the Sharia, or Islamic law, and a military-backed government. Mgr Teissier's courage and desire to stay alongside the Algerian people in their hour of need touched me.

I then forgot about the article and got on with the demands of being school chaplain and living the monastic round. During the school holidays I suddenly felt inspired to write a word of support to Archbishop Teissier. I didn't have his address and just sent my short letter to the Archévêque d'Alger, Alger, Algeria and promptly forgot all about it. To my surprise a few months later a reply arrived written on behalf of the Archbishop by Fr John MacWilliam, a former student of Worth School. I didn't know that Fr John, a White Father, was in Algeria so this added another twist to the plot.

Discovering this unknown link with Algeria whetted my interest. John came to visit Worth School and monastery on a few occasions and so my interest grew. In the summer of 2004 I visited the Tibhirine community which had regrouped in Morocco after the beheading of seven of their members in 1996. Worries about travelling on my own to the unknown world of North Africa were lessening and, encouraged by some of my monastic brethren, I decided that the time was ripe for a visit, or rather a pilgrimage, to the Algerian Church. So I emailed two people in Algiers, putting out feelers about the possibility of spending some time there. The first request received no reply. The second, sent a few weeks later, also drew a blank. The silence was ominous. I decided that I would have to give up this dream as it wasn't meant to be. The Lord wasn't in it. Shortly after resigning myself to not going to Algeria, I received an email from Mgr Teissier inviting me to come and stay with him at the Diocesan House: 'We will welcome you with great joy'. The second person whom I had emailed had forwarded my letter to the Archbishop. So my prayers had been answered but only after I had first accepted an apparent 'No'.

I made my first visit to Algeria in April 2005, and in meeting Mgr Teissier, the people and clergy, I was energized by their love for and warm relationships with their Muslim brothers and sisters. I had drunk at the pure fountain of the Gospel message in all its wonderful

Touched by God

simplicity. A second and more demanding visit followed in March/April 2006. At Archbishop Teissier's suggestion I have written a book[1] about the 19 martyrs, 19 lives freely given out of love for their Muslim brothers and sisters. This contact with a Church of martyrs, a Church which loves and is greatly loved by her Muslim friends, has been a deep source of inspiration for me. I have no idea where this interest will lead as visiting Algeria isn't easy. At the very least my three short visits to North Africa have given me the ability to see Muslims as fellow believers and as brothers and sisters made in the image and likeness of the one God. A monastic vocation can lead you to the most unexpected places!

DRAWING CLOSER TO CHRIST

I have now spent 19 years living the monastic life, trying to learn how 'to put nothing whatever before Christ' (*RB* 72). One of the questions frequently asked of monks and nuns is, 'What do you miss most?' I must confess that nothing springs immediately to mind. It is very easy to idealize life outside the monastery, or inside for that matter. Each life has its own challenges and joys. I try to live in the present moment and rarely think about what I might be doing if I had not chosen to become a monk. However, if I had to give an answer it would be that I miss my country and living near my family. I miss the haunting beauty of the scenery in the West of Ireland where I grew up. The rugged landscapes and unspoilt countryside speak very much of God's presence in his Creation. The Atlantic breakers, the desolate bogs and the lonely mountains all speak of a presence and of a peace. The landscape around Worth is very beautiful but it is also very tame and kept very much under human control. In the West of Ireland the country-

94

side and the surging Atlantic Ocean speak to me much more powerfully of God. And I miss this wildness amidst the tame, pastoral beauty of West Sussex.

The reader may also well wonder how my 19 years at Worth have changed me. I wish I could answer that question clearly and easily. Someone meeting me now would probably be surprised by how little I have changed. And yet the practice of humility, which implies change and growth, is at the heart of the *Rule of St Benedict*, a humility which recognizes our dependence upon God for all that we are and do and involves a willingness to face up to the truth about ourselves. And the community offers the monk or nun a mirror in which we can see more clearly our true selves if we are willing to look in it.

My growth in self-awareness has always been very gradual and I have always been wary, through fear of rejection, about revealing my intimate self to others. Recently, I have become conscious that I am becoming less defensive and a little more self-revelatory in my everyday interactions. This growth in self-acceptance does not necessarily entail a growth in holiness but it certainly provides a more solid foundation upon which grace can build. Being part of a community means that the gifts and insights which I lack can be found in others. Taking up St Paul's metaphor of the Body of Christ in 1 Corinthians, what is important is not having a leading role but rather to put the gifts given to me by the Spirit, however insignificant they may be, at the service of others. The monastery is a school for lifelong learners where each one of us, in the company of brothers or sisters, strives in St Paul's words, 'to put on the likeness of Christ' (cf. 2 Cor. 3.18). We travel *'all together* to everlasting life' (*RB* 72). In helping each other to draw closer to Christ we simultaneously draw closer to each other.

As St Paul makes clear in his First Letter to the Corinthians, the whole point of the Christian life is to grow in our capacity to love, to become more like God. There is of course also in the Bible a stress on obeying the commandments and on acting justly. It seems to me that what holds the various strands of Christian teaching together and makes them life-giving are the central commandments of love of God and love of neighbour. As Cardinal Duval of Algeria has written: 'Justice is necessary to get rid of the causes of poverty in the structures of society. But fraternal love gives justice its vigour and its creative strength. Without love, people lack the imagination to implement justice'.[2] Love is at the heart of the Christian revelation and can be summed up in three words from the First Letter of St John, 'God is love' (1 Jn 4.8). And it is through participating in this divine life, through being taken up into this divine outpouring of love that we begin to understand the meaning and purpose of our own lives.

What I have just written above about love may sound rather abstract and idealistic. One of the attractive features of the *Rule of St Benedict*, however, is its realism. St Benedict has no illusions about human perfectibility and knows that this side of the grave we will continue to struggle with our 'weaknesses of body or of character' (*RB* 72). I find Benedict's realism encouraging because, the longer I spend in the monastery, the more I become aware of my many weaknesses of character. This awareness is humbling and invites me to rely on God's strength and not on my own. It also invites me to have compassion for other people's weaknesses. This does not mean that monastic life is a joyless existence. On the contrary, a sign of the Holy Spirit's presence in our lives is joy even in the midst of difficulties and suffering. The presence of joy is a sure sign that we're not just focusing on ourselves but are allowing the Lord into the interstices of our everyday lives, enabling us to forget self and to go out to others. The words we speak and the life we live ought to speak of someone else, of an indwelling and life-giving Presence at work in and through us. St Benedict in his Prologue tells us that 'as we progress in this way of life and in faith, we shall run on the path of God's commandments, our hearts overflowing with the inexpressible delight of love' (*RB*, Prologue, 49).

A prayer by Br Roger of Taizé which I copied into a notebook a few weeks before my first visit to Worth in 1986 captures the point of it all:

Jesus, Risen Lord, placing our confidence in
you means living in the here and now,
and nowhere else.

Our past lies buried in the heart of God,
and you have already taken care of our future.

When everything urges us to leave you,
you are present. You pray within us, poor and
humble of heart. Ceaselessly you tell us:
'My love for you will never pass away.
And do you love me?'
And we stammer our reply:
'You know I love you.
Perhaps not as I would like to,
but I do love you'.[3]

NOTES

1. M. McGee, *Christian Martyrs for a Muslim People*. Paulist Press, forthcoming.
2. M.-C. Ray (1998), *Le Cardinal Duval*. Paris: Les Éditions du Cerf, p. 46.

3. Brother Roger, (1986), *A Heart that Trusts, Journal 1979–81*. London: Mowbray, p. 120. Reproduced by kind permission of Continuum International Publishing Group.

5

Shopping Around

Alban Hood

'Do monks go shopping?' is a question I am sometimes asked and dread answering, because I am a recovering shopaholic. There are some shops, however, that I try to avoid these days, such as the dry cleaners where I once had an embarrassing experience. Calling there to collect my monk's habit, I was mortified when the assistant enquired: 'Are you going to a fancy dress party or are you in a play?' A little flustered and non-plussed, I heard myself reply: 'Oh, no, I'm for real!' It was only after I had left the shop and was walking down the street that it occurred to me that my response had been rather arrogant. Could I actually claim to be 'for real'? Who is the real me? I may look like a monk from the outside, but do my inner motivations match up? As I look back on my life so far, I realize how tortuous that quest for one's true identity can be.

STRAWBERRY JAM ON BURNT TOAST

I was born in Cheshire on 12 March 1962 and was baptized on Easter Sunday the same year. My parents had met while members of the youth club attached to the Congregational Church where they were later married and I was baptized. By the time my sister was born, in December 1964, my parents had become Methodists, and so early memories of church are of Sunday school, hymn-singing and the rather musty smell of the building. As a child of the 60s, I grew up with programmes such as *Thunderbirds* and *Star Trek* and, mesmerized by television pictures of the Apollo space missions, it was perhaps inevitable that I pictured our Lord's ascension as a kind of 'divine lift-off'. Childhood constructs can be facile and crude but they stay with us for a long time. I remember as a small child being terrified by the huge radio telescope at nearby Jodrell Bank which dominated the Cheshire plain and made me aware of the immensity of the universe. A love of music featured in my life from early on. Aged 5, I began to play the piano 'by ear' and soon developed a very catholic taste in music, ranging from Dvorak's *New World Symphony* to George Harrison's 'My Sweet Lord', which was the first record I bought at the age of 9.

Moving house became a feature of my childhood. On account of my father's job we moved south twice, first to Leicestershire, and then, when I was 10, to Hertfordshire, to a picturesque village perched on the edge of the Chilterns. The nearest Methodist church was some miles away and, encouraged by the young vicar, we began to attend the village parish church, where I joined the choir. It was there that I began to develop my love of music and worship, assisted by what the vicar called 'strawberry jam on burnt toast' – the red coloured *Hymns Ancient and Modern* which, in every pew in church, had to be placed on top of the black *Book of Common Prayer*. At the time I loved the 'strawberry jam' of the melodious hymn tunes but found the 'burnt toast' of the language of the 1662 Prayer Book harder to stomach, although later I grew to love the collects at Evensong, especially the one that began 'Lighten our darkness we beseech thee, O Lord ...' I was confirmed at the age of 14 by the future Archbishop of Canterbury, Robert Runcie, in a local Anglo-Catholic church. I loved the ritual and the music there and found our village church worship bland and unexciting in comparison, although I was moved by the experience of serving the early morning Communion service celebrated with great devotion by a retired clergyman. I learned by heart the lovely prayer he always recited when we returned to the vestry after the service, a prayer I later discovered to be the opening prayer of the Mass of the Feast of Corpus Christi. The 'strawberry jam' of church music continued to nourish me, and at the age of 14, I became the organist of a nearby village church. At 16 I began formal organ lessons at St Alban's Abbey and soon developed affection for the cathedral and its saint, whose name I was later to take.

PATH TO ROME

In March 1978 I took part in a school holiday to Rome, a surprising destination given that the school had no particular religious affiliation and made no provision for Latin in the curriculum. From the very first, I found Rome a most appealing place, romantic and steeped in history. The sight of the ailing Pope Paul VI, standing at the window of the papal palace evoked new thought and awareness of the Roman Catholic Church. On my return from Rome I devoured every Catholic book I could find, in search of some explanation about the body which claimed to be the one authentic communion of Christ. 1978 was the 'Year of Three Popes', beginning with the death of Pope Paul on 6 August. My interest in the Catholic Church was still an intellectual one, but I was already being drawn interiorly to the religious life through a TV documentary about St Thérèse of Lisieux, the French Carmelite nun. She provided a model of faith and prayer through which I came to appreciate that the one is meaningless without the other. I began to see how a life can be touched and shaped by the love of God if one is open and receptive.

Not long after my seventeenth birthday, a short story I had written won me a place, with 50 other 'A'-level students, on an all-expenses paid tour of Europe which began in London and ended in Venice. The first day's adventures on this 'Grand Tour' included a visit to Westminster Abbey. I remember asking the way to that other Westminster which lay at the end of Victoria Street, and so it was that I entered the Byzantine-style cathedral and sat in the hushed, dark silence in the shadow of the huge, suspended crucifix above the sanctuary. I knelt and prayed, and after a while became aware of another's presence, kneeling beside me. I looked up from my folded hands to see – nothing. Yet I had the sense of someone there, close by. Many years later I discovered the following passage in Antonia White's *The Lost Traveller* which recaptured that experience in Westminster Cathedral:

Slowly the faint thawing warmth grew in his heart
as if someone, far away down a long passage,
were bringing a light ... Then he became aware,
not with his mind or his sense but with some faculty
never awakened before, of an intense personal presence
in the church.[1]

Then, what sounded like a heavenly choir burst forth from a side chapel where Vespers was beginning. I sat enthralled for some minutes, genuflected and left hurriedly, for I had the curious sense of needing to escape. A priest standing at the back of the cathedral approached me to ask if I was OK but I passed by, picking up on my way out a card which read 'The Truth about the Catholic Church'. A few months later a local Catholic priest asked if I would be willing to become organist at his church. I agreed, and at the beginning of 1980, took up my new duties. From the outset I loved the Sunday High Mass with its ceremonies and Gregorian chant. The parish priest was a genial Cumbrian who readily answered my questions and lent me his books. One morning after Mass he remarked: 'I think you're going to make a very fine priest one day.' I replied that first I would have to become a Catholic. Eight months later, on Saturday, 20 September 1980, I was received into the Catholic Church. My family coped quite well with this decision; only later did I learn that many of my Glasgow forebears had been members of the Orange Lodge!

LIVERPOOL AND POPE JOHN PAUL II

Christ's and Notre Dame College was the amalgamation of two Catholic teacher training colleges in the leafy suburbs of South Liverpool, and it was here, two days after my reception into the Catholic Church, that I began a four-year course in History and American Studies. Although I enjoyed the studies, this period of my life was more significant for the foundations that were laid for my future vocation. I lived in a hall of residence next to the college chapel where I joined a small group that met for Morning and Evening Prayer each day. I had already purchased a shiny new weekday missal and daily Mass became a regular part of my life. And then there were my feeble attempts at meditation each morning before lectures began. The important thing, though, was that I was beginning to desire to lead a genuinely prayerful life. In May 1982 Pope John Paul II made a pastoral visit to Britain, and I became involved in the preparations for the Liverpool events

103

through a part-time job in the Liverpool Archdiocesan Press Office. On the day itself I worked as a reporter for the local Catholic newspaper and was stationed in the press stand outside Liverpool's Anglican Cathedral where the Pope was greeted by rapturous applause. The papal visit highlighted two important aspects of my future life: an interest in journalism and a deepening awareness of a vocation to the priesthood.

Although I had read and been inspired by *The Seven Storey Mountain*, the autobiography of the American monk Thomas Merton, I did not at this stage seriously consider the monastic life – that seemed too final, too much of a commitment. Looking back at my diary, I can see that I was periodically beset by a strong pull to the priesthood which seemed to induce an inner turmoil. I would be troubled by insomnia and would spend hours walking through a local park in the middle of the night. It was at these times that I felt most alone and isolated, while paradoxically wanting to spend long hours in prayer. After meeting Cardinal Basil Hume when he came on a visitation to our parish in Hertfordshire, I read his book *Searching for God*,[2] which made a deep impression on me, and introduced me to the English Benedictines who live in monasteries but also do pastoral work outside. I was attracted by Hume's assertion that it was possible for a monk to live in the 'market-place' of parishes and schools as well as in the 'desert' of silence and solitude. Early in 1981 I responded to an advertisement for a vocations retreat at St Augustine's Abbey, Ramsgate. It was the start of a four-year journey.

SHOPPING AROUND

It was perhaps inevitable that this shopaholic should adopt marketplace strategies in discerning his vocation. All along I struggled with the conflicting attractions of monastery or diocese. Should I become a monk or a priest serving in a diocese? I made contact with the vocations director in Westminster diocese and met with him regularly at Allen Hall, the diocesan seminary in Chelsea. I also visited a number of monasteries: Ramsgate, Ampleforth, Ealing and Belmont. Both at Allen Hall and at each of the monasteries I was made very welcome and continued to correspond with the people I met there for many years afterwards. The conflict between diocesan priesthood and monastic life seemed to be resolved when I discovered Ealing Abbey, a small monastic community in West London which also ran a day school and a busy parish. I sensed Ealing might offer just what I was looking for, a monastery which represented a 'desert' in the heart of a busy urban 'marketplace'.

I would say that discovering Ealing Abbey was the turning point in my monastic journey, at least in providing a place to discern more deeply. I already knew something about the monastery at Ealing through Dom John Main who had opened a centre for Christian Meditation there in the 1970s and whose writings were becoming very popular by the early 1980s. In the summer before he died John Main had come to my college in Liverpool to give a talk which inspired me to join a local meditation group and begin to meditate each day. Gradually this discipline changed my life and I became less restless and agitated about my future and settled down to prepare for my Finals. While I sensed that the monastic life was where my future lay, I thought it would be best to gain some experience of the world of work before entering. My love of writing suggested a career in journalism, and, helped by some work experience at the local Catholic newspaper and at the Liverpool Archdiocesan Press Office, I secured a job as a trainee reporter at a national Catholic newspaper in London where my first task was to do a story on the fire at York Minster. At weekends I would often stay at Ealing Abbey and it soon became obvious to me that I was not suited to the world of journalism. After only a few months in the job I resigned and, at the suggestion of the abbot, went to live at Ealing for a month to discern whether I had a vocation to the monastic life. The monks were very kind to me and it seemed that I had found the place where God wanted me to be. It was agreed that I should return in January and make a formal application to enter the monastery. A friend advised caution, and suggested that I visit another monastery before I made my decision.

DANCING MONKS

It was a cold Saturday morning in December 1984 when I first arrived at Douai Abbey. From its name, I had thought the abbey was in France, so had eliminated it from my shopping list, but a friend told me it was near Reading in Berkshire. In 1984 the Abbey comprised a hotchpotch of buildings, dominated by the Gothic-style Abbey Church which had been built, but not completed, in the 1930s. The Lady Chapel and the central crossing were the only part of architect Arnold Crush's plan that had been executed, leaving a high, truncated building which dominated the beautiful surrounding countryside. Entering the church, I was struck by its high, clear glass windows through which the December sun shone brightly. The monastery buildings, designed by Sir Frederick Gibberd, the architect of the Catholic cathedral in Liverpool, were spacious and well-planned. The school attached to the monastery was small in comparison to its Benedictine counterparts at Ampleforth and Downside and then contained 300 pupils. Douai had plenty of vocations at the time – I think there were 12 junior monks in December 1984, most of them in their 20s and 30s, and there was an atmosphere of hope and vitality. This obviously had an impact on me, for I jotted down in my notebook some words from Jean Vanier to the effect that when we are deeply attracted by the people who live in a community it is perhaps a sign that we too are called to enter into the same sort of covenant. Certainly the place had many attractions: the setting, the friendliness of the brethren, the liturgy, and the fact that the young monks seemed to have so much fun. After Compline on that first evening, I was invited down to the school refectory where a barn dance was in full swing, and, to my amazement, I recognized some of the dancers as young monks who a short time before had been in church! I can't begin to describe the strong pull the place exerted on me – it was a sort of home-coming. I knew then that I could never join the community at Ealing, and that if I had a vocation to the monastic life it would be as a monk of Douai.

Early in the New Year I made a difficult visit to Ealing to tell the abbot and the novice master of my changed plans, and was moved by their gracious response. On 31 January, I returned to Douai and the next day had a long talk with one of the junior monks, which affected me deeply. We went for a walk through the abbey gardens and, pausing to sit by the small pond, looked back at the glorious view of the Abbey Church, its windows gleaming in the winter sun. As the monk spoke about the joys and the struggles of the monastic life, warmth filled my heart and I realized that the life of a monk at Douai was what I was searching for. That afternoon I went to see the novice master and within a month I had made a formal application to join the community. But first I had to spend a trial month living inside the monastery. It took a while to adjust to the rhythm of the monastic day and the less palatable elements of the routine, especially housework and gardening, but my memories of this month are happy and rosy ones of getting to know some of the community and the countryside around the monastery. This was an experience so different from the month spent at Ealing. From the very start I felt rooted at Douai, aided no doubt by the warm welcome from the community and especially from the younger members. During this month there were hints of some of the problems I was to face later on, such as loneliness, the struggle of personal prayer and a lack of self-confidence, but in the main it was a happy and positive time and I left secure in the knowledge that Douai and I were compatible. On 3 July 1985, the Feast of St Thomas, the Abbot's Council accepted me for the novitiate for September. Looking back, I am amazed at the speed with which all this took place: by the time I entered the monastery I had known the community for barely nine months.

THE BEST IS YET TO BE

It was a sunny morning in late August 1985 when I left home to begin my novitiate with three others at Douai. Of the original group, only two of us have survived in monastic life. We were clothed by Abbot Gregory Freeman on Sunday 1 September and, most unusually, permission had been given for our families to attend the ceremony which is traditionally witnessed only by the monastic community. At the end of the ceremony we were each given a new name: I became Brother Alban – reflecting my love for Hertfordshire and the cathedral which had so many important associations for me. Saying goodbye to my parents and sister was a traumatic experience, for the novice master had decreed that the novices were not to be allowed family visits for 12 months. This was to prove a painful issue for both the family and myself and I was to suffer from homesickness for much of my first year in the monastery.

Life in the novitiate was very ordered and circumscribed. We rose at 6 a.m. and after the Morning Office, meditation, Mass and breakfast, had to spend an hour of prayerful scripture reading (*lectio divina*) before classes with the novice master at 10 a.m. After a coffee break, which we had to take by ourselves and not with the community, we had another class, Scripture or Liturgy with one of the other monks, or Monastic History with the abbot. After Midday Prayer and lunch we had two hours of manual labour which involved cleaning, gardening or chopping logs for the big fire in the calefactory or common room. This was the most difficult period of the day for someone like me who hated practical work of any sort. After tea with the community in the refectory there was time for exercise (often swimming in the school pool) before meditation in church together before Vespers. Again this proved a difficulty for me as I often fell asleep and on more than one occasion woke to find myself still sitting in the nave of the Abbey Church while the community was beginning to sing Latin Vespers in choir. Supper in the refectory then followed, a formal occasion with a monk serving the meal to the community while another read aloud, usually from a work of history or a biography. The book being read at the time I entered was a biography of Cardinal Manning. After supper there was compulsory recreation in the calefactory where the community met to talk for half-an-hour or so. There was then free time for letter-writing or reading before Compline at 9.30 p.m. after which we were all forbidden to talk and came out of the church with the hoods of our habits up. It was a long day and falling asleep was never too much of a problem.

On the first Wednesday of every month we had what was

called a 'month day' when there was talking at meals and we were allowed to go out from after breakfast until Vespers. Usually as novices we had to spend this day out together, with the princely sum of £3 each to spend. Sometimes, however, we did manage to escape on our own. In those days we were lucky to be taken out by other members of the community, either to visit other monasteries or to local places of interest. West Berkshire is a lovely part of the world and is at its best in the autumn. I loved exploring local lanes and villages, either on foot or by bicycle. Community life within the strict framework of the novitiate soon proved to be a great trial, especially living in such proximity to other people whose attitudes and behaviour can so easily grate, so these days out were important oases.

My novitiate year was dominated by a powerful inner struggle – I had thought myself fairly mature and self-aware at the age of 23, but soon realized how much I had to learn about myself and my emotions. Thankfully, there were some good and sane guides to help and support me. I will always be grateful for the excellent spiritual formation I received in the novitiate. We were given particularly sound training in the monastic art of *lectio divina* – the prayerful reading of the Scriptures and other spiritual works and I gained a great deal from this discipline. I returned time and again to two favourite passages: the first from the book of Exodus (14.14) where Moses says to the people: 'the Lord will fight for you, and you have only to be still'; and the second which begins 'My son, if you come forward to serve the Lord, prepare yourself for temptation ... do not be hasty in time of calamity ... Cleave to him and do not depart' (Sir. 2.1-3). These two texts sustained and nourished me in those early months.

The winter of 1985–1986 was a hard and bleak one and spring seemed a long time in coming. At times I felt

110

desperately lonely and misunderstood and was often ill. I lost a lot of weight and old problems with possessiveness in human relationships continued so that by Easter both the abbot and novice master openly expressed doubts about my suitability for the monastic life. My parents came to visit me in March and pleaded with me to leave if I was unhappy, which at the time I certainly was. I sensed that whatever else I did, it would be important to keep going until the end of the novitiate year. It has been my experience that God always sends help when we need it, but often in surprising guises. Help arrived in the form of two members of the community, one young and one old. The first was a parish father who came to talk to the novices about life on a parish. He impressed me by his honesty, humour and openness and afterwards I asked to see him. He encouraged me to persevere, and to confide in a friend of his in the resident community. It proved to be a wise choice. My other mentor was at that time the oldest member of the community: Father Sylvester Mooney celebrated his centenary in June 1986. He had been Abbot of Douai for 40 years (1929–69) and was a source of inspiration to many. He spoke of events like the sinking of the *Titanic* in 1912 as if they were yesterday. We novices were required to assist him in getting to the church and the refectory, to serve his private Mass and to say Compline with him after putting him to bed. Such was the impact of his presence that I felt able to confide in him concerning my temptations to leave the monastery. He told me of the time not long after he was elected Abbot. Feeling burdened and disillusioned, he was walking outside the front of the monastery and looked across the Kennet valley to the Hampshire downs (still a glorious view today), when he saw a vision of the valley filled with water and a boat bobbing up and down on the water. On its sail were written some words taken from a poem by Robert

Browning: 'grow old along with me, the best is yet to be'. That vision inspired me, as it still does, and after that, although I had many (increasingly more serious) temptations to leave the monastery in later years, I persevered to make my first Profession of Vows in October 1986 and, in January 1990, my Solemn (or Final) Profession.

OXFORD AND LIBERATION

Although I did not shine academically at school, I enjoyed studying, especially History and Literature. My headmaster did not consider me bright enough to go to university, and I rather fulfilled his prophecy by poor 'A'-level grades which scuppered entry to my chosen course at Manchester University. I went on to obtain a good Honours degree from Liverpool, but it was a General Arts degree that took four, and not the usual three, years to complete. I felt I could achieve better. One of the community encouraged me to begin historical research and I produced two articles that were published in *The Douai Magazine*. Study provided an anchor for me in my first two difficult years in the monastery and I found I had an aptitude for it. I was thrilled, therefore, when Abbot Gregory told me that he wanted me to go to Oxford to read for a degree in Theology. I had been given a chance to redeem myself. St Benet's Hall is a Permanent Private Hall of the University owned by Ampleforth Abbey. It had originally been founded to enable Benedictine monks to obtain degrees in order to teach in the schools attached to the monasteries. The monastic regime at St Benet's was relaxed. Morning Prayer was at 7 a.m. but there was no formal prayer at the end of the day, and after dinner and recreation we were free to do as we wished, even visit local pubs which was something novices were forbidden to do at Douai. I also made friends in the wider world of the University. After the enclosed world of the novitiate, Oxford for me was a place of liberation. Guest nights, to which tutors from Blackfriars and the University colleges were invited, were usually looked forward to as especially convivial occasions.

At Oxford I worked hard, but also played hard. I wanted to be with the 'sinners' in the pub at night, but I also wanted to be up early with the 'saints' in the chapel in the morning. The Oxford term was short, only 8 weeks, and sometimes we would be required to write two essays a week. Tutorials, one-to-one with a tutor, were demanding experiences when it would be very clear whether or not the student had read the books on the reading list. The summer term was always glorious; work was often forsaken in favour of punting trips down the river or afternoons spent in the University Parks or the local beer gardens. I would return to the monastery for occasional weekends during term, but for the most part was allowed to stay in Oxford to study. After graduating, I remained at St Benet's Hall for a further year to undertake pastoral studies at Blackfriars, and then went on to St Mary's College, Strawberry Hill, Twickenham, to obtain my Postgraduate Certificate in Education, as the abbot decided that my future lay in the school at Douai.

FINAL VOWS AND ORDINATION

A few months before Finals at Oxford, I made my permanent commitment as a monk by taking Final, or Solemn Vows. I find it extraordinary now that at the time I made this important step, I was away from the monastery for most of the year, and had no experience of the major works of the community, neither the school nor the parishes. Nevertheless, on 6 January 1990, as the litany of saints was chanted during the Solemn Profession ceremony, my novitiate contemporary and I lay on the black funeral pall as a symbol that we were dying to worldliness and being raised to new life with Christ. Later that day, our hoods were pinned up (while we were still wearing them) and we observed three liturgical days of silence. It was a blissful time and also a time of new hope for the community which had lost two abbots in 12 months. The new abbot, Leonard Vickers, although a Douai monk, was Abbot of St Anselm's, Washington DC at the time of his election as our abbot. Personable, direct and very human, he soon won hearts and minds and injected into the community a sense of new purpose. With such an atmosphere in the air it was relatively easy for me to make a permanent commitment to the community. It was, therefore, a devastating blow when one September afternoon Abbot Leonard was suddenly taken from us by a fatal heart attack at the early age of 55. I couldn't believe it – when all seemed to be looking so positive and bright, the Lord took from us the man who seemed to be the only one capable of reversing our fortunes. I began to see my Solemn Profession as a mistake: I had put my trust in a man, not in God who alone could save me. It was a painful lesson to learn but I clung to those words of the *Suscipe,* the verse from Psalm 118[119] (v. 116) that Benedictines sing at their Solemn Profession of final vows and which I had sung just eight months before:

If you uphold me by your promise, I shall live;
Let my hopes not be in vain.

Before his death, Abbot Leonard had fixed the date for my ordination as a deacon, which took place in December 1990. A year later, on 21 December 1991, I was ordained to the priesthood.

IDENTITY CRISIS

Even from the time before I joined the monastery I have struggled with the tension between priesthood and monastic life, or, to use Cardinal Hume's phrase quoted earlier, the conflict between being in the 'desert' and working in the 'marketplace'. It is sometimes said that the male English Benedictine vocation is a 'fudge', an unsatisfactory amalgam of two contrasting lifestyles, the monastic and the missionary. St Benedict himself was probably not an ordained priest and it seems he did not envisage that many of his monks would be priests either. Yet, when the English Benedictine Congregation (EBC) was re-founded in the seventeenth century, the pope entrusted the monks with the task of working on the English mission, and of sustaining the faith of persecuted English Catholics. Until the twentieth century English Benedictine monks were required to take an oath in which they promised to go on the English mission if they were requested to do so. Although to date I have spent most of my monastic life away from the monastery in pastoral work, I wasn't initially very comfortable with the practicalities of being a monk-priest. The Douai community has a strong mission tradition but initially I questioned the value of serving parishes far away from the monastery, when the monks serving them only returned once or twice a year, or in some cases once every eight years for an abbatial election. There were characters one heard about but never saw; legendary stories of monks who swapped parishes with each other without informing the abbot or the bishop. It is so easy to forget that the essence of the monastic vocation is a call to life in common, not ordination. It seemed to me that in some cases our traditional Benedictine parishes came to replicate diocesan parish life rather than bringing to these parishes the spirit of St Benedict. On the other side there

115

were those whom I regarded as heroes, monks who were able to live the conventual life and be good missioners on the parishes. There was always the impressive example set by Fathers who had spent many years on parishes, and were then able to settle back contentedly into conventual life in the monastery.

By the mid-1990s I was beginning to suffer from an identity crisis: at first I had enjoyed teaching but it wasn't long before I discovered how soul-destroying can be the task of teaching Religious Education to uninterested adolescent boys (at least unless you have a special gift for teaching). At the time the community was severely tried by a series of departures and scandals, and the school was in decline. I began to question the wisdom of monks running a school where they were easily distracted from the regular round of the Divine Office and community life. But there was a more fundamental identity crisis going on deep within myself as increasingly I found that the monastic life, like burnt toast, can be hard and unpalatable. I observed with some envy my married friends having babies and my priest friends acquiring their first parishes. I found regular prayer impossible and increasingly looked forward to any excuse to get out of the monastery. The heart seemed to have gone out of my vocation. Eventually Fr Abbot and his Council agreed that I needed time out and allowed me a year's sabbatical. I was to live on one of the monastery's parishes in Lancashire and do some basic training as a counsellor before returning to Douai.

LIFE IN THE MARKETPLACE

I was indeed to spend the next seven years living in a marketplace, for Ormskirk is a Lancashire town famous for its market, a place with long-established Benedictine connections going back to the eighteenth century. The Catholic parish of St Anne is a thriving community which in the mid-1990s had a Sunday Mass attendance of around 800 people, a high degree of lay involvement and a large number of parish groups and societies. When I arrived there were two monks serving the parish, assisted by three married permanent deacons. Besides two convents, there were three schools, a busy general hospital and a large parochial club next door to the modern priory where the monks lived. Lancashire folk are forthright but friendly and I was soon made very welcome, even though to begin with my involvement in the parish was limited. I assisted with Masses and helped with the confirmation programme. However, within a year I was appointed curate and the following year unexpectedly became parish priest. At the age of 35 and with very little parochial experience, I found myself heading one of the major parishes in the diocese. The learning curve was very steep. Looking back, it was providential that I did some training as a counsellor at Manchester University because the course taught me some useful listening skills and provided a framework for pastoral work.

A shy person, I found large parish events quite stressful but endeavoured to put into practice some advice from the vicar who had prepared me for confirmation. He told me once that he thought a parish priest should aim to 'touch the lives of many people as lightly as possible'. I encouraged parishioners with particular gifts to provide the expertise I lacked, particularly in financial and personnel matters. One of my first initiatives was to form a Parish Pastoral Council that was representative of the different age groups and interests of the community. Although I always tried to be courteous and patient, I made a number of mistakes in dealing with people and was not always successful in

117

winning them over to accept a different outlook on parish issues. At times I found parishioners' expectations of their parish priest unrealistic and unreasonable and always found confrontation difficult. But I was blessed with the support of many parishioners as well as the friendship and co-operation of the clergy team. It was a tremendous privilege to live with two other monks who were able to enjoy each other's company and offer mutual support. One of the most satisfying parish projects was the launching of a major church refurbishment appeal which spawned a whole variety of fund-raising events from concerts and quiz nights to fêtes and dances. In the interests of the appeal, I conquered my fear of heights by being sponsored to climb a local church tower and brave a popular local roller-coaster ride that was appropriately named 'the traumatizer'.

Parish life was busy but fulfilling and at times baffling as I struggled to provide pastoral support for the dying and the bereaved. A high point of my time in Ormskirk was the celebration of the millennium which coincided with celebrations for the 150th anniversary of the opening of the church. These were happy years when I felt fulfilled and discovered how the different vocations of the monk and the priest complemented each other. In particular, and somewhat paradoxically perhaps, I began to value the monastery and the Benedictine vocation: so much so that I was inspired to articulate a vision of how parish life could be based on the principles of the *Rule of Saint Benedict* with its major themes of prayer, community and study. The result was a document entitled 'A Benedictine Vision' which was circulated around the parish and later published, in summary form, in *The Benedictine Yearbook*.[3]

SEARCHING FOR 'DISCIPLINED INTIMACY'

For a few years I felt at a distance from what was going on back in the monastery and my visits to Douai were infrequent. However, in 1998 I was elected to the Abbot's Council which necessitated regular trips down to Berkshire and helped me to re-integrate into the life of the community. I came to see how much I missed the monastic liturgy, especially Gregorian chant. As the pressures of parish life increased, I began to appreciate the Benedictine balance of prayer, work and study and felt keenly the need for more prayer and study. In 1999 I started work on a doctorate in Church History which provided a much-needed interest outside parish life. The tenor of my personal life in these years was summed up by the title of a dissertation I wrote for my counselling diploma: 'Searching for disciplined intimacy', a study of the relationship between the monastic vows and the principles of person-centred counselling. For so long I had sought love in all the wrong places, from those who were quite unable to give it, or whose gift was not meant for me. It has taken me a long time to learn not to experience those sorts of situation as a rejection, and to learn, rather, to receive and enjoy the love I already have. During my Ormskirk years I was in therapy. The main question that seemed to be addressed was how my affective needs could be met appropriately. It took me all of those seven years and more to realize that my needs had already been met, whether I was aware of it or not, by my family, friends and monastic brethren. Over the years I've come to appreciate that the gifts we seek are not always those that God desires us to receive, and those that we do receive we do not always appreciate. I also began to learn not to regard my failings negatively, not to see them as dead-ends, but instead as avenues for new growth, since, as

119

Cardinal Newman asserted: 'It is by God's Providence that we succeed by failure.' Reflecting on this period of my life, I detect a gradual gravitation back to the monastery, so that when, after seven years, the abbot asked me to return there, I willingly complied, although I was daunted by the prospect of becoming novice master with the responsibility of forming others in the monastic life.

My seven years away from the monastery certainly equipped me with new skills and experience, for which I will always be grateful. As I look back over the first 22 years of my monastic life, among the greatest gifts I have received are human support and a growth in self-confidence. Being nurtured in a monastic climate has certainly allowed hidden gifts to flourish, such as the aptitude for study that led to the achievement of a doctorate despite early setbacks. These days I worry less about whether or not I am a 'real monk' and strive instead to accept the person I am with all my strengths and weaknesses. I rejoice in the balance and wisdom of the Benedictine tradition, which ensures 'that the strong are challenged and the feeble are not overwhelmed' (*RB* 64:19).[4] What matters is not what I am trying to do for God but what God does for me in loving me and sustaining me in my search for him in the Benedictine way. It has taken me a long time to realize that self-seeking never leads to the discovery of one's true self, for it is only in seeking God that we find ourselves. There are still bad days when I want to give it all up, but these days the grass in other places seems no longer as green as once it did. I still enjoy shopping when the opportunity arises, but over the past few years I have come to really believe the old adage that 'happiness means not having what you want, but wanting what you have'. Since returning to the monastery I sense that I am not as restless as I was, but maybe I have come to see that restlessness is not a wholly undesirable state, as it can spur us on in our journey and encourage us to reflect on what it is that we are seeking, for as St Augustine's famous prayer reminds us: 'You have made us for yourself, O Lord, and our hearts are restless until they find rest in you.'[5]

NOTES

1. A. White (1979), *The Lost Traveller*. London: Virago Press.
2. G. B. Hume (1977), *Searching for God*. London: Hodder & Stoughton.
3. 'A Benedictine Vision for a Benedictine Parish', *The Benedictine and Cistercian Monastic Yearbook 2000*. The EBC Trust, p. 36.
4. T. G. Kardong (1996), *Benedict's Rule: A Translation and Commentary*. Collegeville: The Liturgical Press, p. 527.
5. St Augustine, *Confessions*, Book I.1.

6

In the Middle of Life's Journey

David Foster

Run and do now what will profit us forever
(RB, Prologue, 44)

It came in a flash, my decision that I had to try my vocation at Downside, a flash of anger. I had finally gone to the Oxford Appointments Committee Offices, as the University Careers Service was known in 1979. For a whole year I had done nothing about it, presumably because I could not really face coming clean about life after Oxford. In the end a final demand arrived rather like a gas bill – or that's how it felt. So I turned up. They asked me the irritating questions about my name, date of birth (back in 1955), college (Corpus Christi) and degree programme (Classics) they already had on their database, and said I should become an accountant. Just like that. I didn't even have any real idea what that was, except that it involved maths, about which I never had much confidence, and had not studied for seven years. I was wondering about becoming a solicitor like my father. That was swept aside with the unforgettable but decisive words 'Oh, there are far too many of those.' So that was that.

122

By the time I got back to Corpus I was in a terrible temper, had a stiff drink, and suddenly things came clear: first, how ridiculous the incident had been; second, that I really did not have any career I really wanted to do; third, that whatever I did I would never be happy until I had tried things out at Downside. That was how I made my decision, or rather how I found it.

It did not, of course, come out of the blue. I had been staying there for a few days in vacations for the previous three years, ostensibly to get on with some study, and other times when I needed to get away. Certainly the place had grown on me, as had the handful of monks I had got to know. What I had grown to love were, in fact, things that really mattered: people's courtesy, humour and attentiveness; their culture and love of learning, but not as I had known it in Oxford, where it so often seemed blemished by a measure of vanity or affectation; here it was woven into a whole way of life centred on God, and something they were trying to share with the school and all comers.

I had visited a couple of other monasteries too, which I had concluded previously were where I should have had to go if I were really called to be a monk; but one was Mirfield and I had become a Roman Catholic; and Quarr Abbey, I had been sure, was too austere and enclosed for me. I did not feel too sure about celibacy either, so avoided thinking about the priesthood. I really did think I should like to be a solicitor like my father. That afternoon of decision, I was still not sure I was called to be a monk, but I could acknowledge that Downside was a fine group of people who were trying, in their own way, to live an integrally Christian way of life, with prayer at the centre of everything, and to live it for others. It had become a very important place for me. Schooled as I had been at King Edward's Birmingham with its noble tradition of Anglican piety and education, I could recognize at Downside the humanist unity of godliness and good learning that had become important to me over my early life. Whatever it was at Downside, I knew I had to give it a go. In a sense I realized I had fallen in love.

DISCOVERING THE NEED TO PRAY

That is the short version of the story. The longer version goes back to my first year at Oxford when I discovered everything in my religious formation going into a melting pot. There should have been nothing surprising about that, but whereas many seemed to relish the freedom, it had a profoundly disturbing effect on me. The first problem was that I did not find a place of worship where I could feel at home, however attractive in different ways they all were. It was the first time I had been away from home and the loss of stable religious co-ordinates threw everything into a mess. My own needs were changing too. Above all I discovered I needed to pray.

Not that I didn't have a habit of prayer. But it no longer counted for anything. That was my first and only 'religious experience', a completely unnerving sense of the emptiness of my life such as it was, and worse, of the absence of God; but I have never been more sure of his reality and that I had to pray as I did not yet know how to. I was walking up towards St Hugh's College by the University Parks in a winter night towards the end of my first term; the stars were clear and it was a beautiful sight but for once more chillingly distant than ever ... But who could I talk to? That was when I realized that the people in college with whom I felt I could best share that kind of need were Catholics. However imperfect they felt their practice of the faith to be, they were not fazed by someone needing to pray, or asking them about prayer, and they just put me straight in touch with one of the Catholic chaplains.

Vocation stirs in many ways in different people. I started in a vague kind of way wanting to be an Anglican priest. That obviously went down the tube when I became a Catholic at the start of my second year in 1976. But one of the big factors in making that move was this need for prayer that had grown in me, a kind of desperate need to get God really at the centre of my life. At Corpus Christi College I found myself working hard, but living a rather incoherent life; existentially rather than morally, though there is much then of which I am not proud. I once heard it described as the bleary semi-consciousness of *l'homme moyen sensuel*. But in spite of this, the need for prayer became suddenly absolutely clear, a demand that gave me a strange kind of joy, even though everything was so much of a muddle.

So the discovery of contemplative prayer was the big thing. And as I discovered a need for silence, I also found places where I could be quiet, places where I could find strength, and increasingly a sense of orientation. The first monastery I visited was the Anglican community at Mirfield, but Quarr and Downside followed in rapid succession. I had never really understood that these kind of places still existed. For me they were places, as T. S. Eliot puts it in *Little Gidding*, a poem that meant a lot to me at the time, where prayer has been valid. They were places where people seemed to know how to live, and places where I found I could begin to put my life together. The metaphors that proved invaluable at that time were navigational, the stability that comes from a ship's deep keel and the idea of a magnetic north which, however wobbly the compass point, helps it settle and makes it possible to find directions.

Among the books that really spoke to me were some reflections by a Carthusian in *They Speak by Silences*. In fact the title really said it all. And then, when I was at Mirfield, I came across a book about Charles de Foucauld by René

125

Voillaume. Suddenly here was a person who had taken the Gospel dead seriously and tried to live it out in solitude and prayer: he identified with the hidden years of our Lord. It has always impressed me about Catholicism that it takes sanctity seriously as involving sacrifice and renunciation. And it expects saints to emerge in every generation. It is a faith that has ambitions for its people. I like that.

POINTERS

I had met a wonderful old man in Oxford for whom St Francis was absolutely real. He had been a married, Baptist minister, but once Catholic acted at the Chaplaincy as a kind of spiritual godfather to people who were trying to take faith seriously. He did a lot to help me focus on vocation and keep it in the picture even when things were not so saintly! He made sanctity credibly human. There is a lot of Francis in Charles de Foucauld, but Charles was a hermit (or became one, having started as a Trappist). Here it was, total dedication like Francis, who is so accessible a saint, but to monastic and contemplative life. For me it was just obviously the way to do it, if that was the way for me. I read a lot about Charles and other books by Voillaume. And then I had to wake up to the fact I could never live so radical a life. It was good that some did – I needed that kind of witness. I simply was not physically up to it (or emotionally, I would have now to add). But de Foucauld had had to change plans too, and in going to North Africa he was seeking his vocation along a path that corresponded to his earlier natural gifts and life as a soldier and explorer. It was his incredible openness to the Spirit, and the complete spontaneity of his passion for Christ, that made that path a path of holiness.

Charles de Foucauld was the great inspiration of that time. But I also came across Thomas Merton, whose own

126

humanity shines through a passion for authenticity centred in contemplative prayer that still compels me; other reading began taking me towards English Benedictinism. Above all, I read the *Cloud of Unknowing* with its simple teaching that we can love God even when he completely exceeds our capacity to know and understand him; and that the sense of darkness and difficulty we have in prayer is not because we have got a problem, but simply because God is not anything we can think of. The same teaching, of course, was implicit in the *Spiritual Letters* of John Chapman, whose 'pray as you can and not as you can't' helped me get less fussed about prayer, especially when it feels like a blank; and finally, I came across Augustine Baker's *Holy Wisdom*. I realized I had been shown a battered copy of this book by an old lady in my Anglican parish at home, for whom it was her greatest treasure. But then I found it in a bookshop myself, and could hardly put it down. As I have said, I was very much in the doldrums about vocation, but all this was still part of the picture, very much so.

And I began to appreciate that I had to be realistic about myself – which so often means, but does not need to mean, that one has to make compromises, or settle for second best. Rather wonderfully, and quite peacefully, I recognized that it was OK to think about Benedictine monasticism, even in the less obviously rigorous style I had come across at Downside (it does have its rigours, of course – all true monastic life does). On the contrary, it was a place where I could certainly use my talents (as I saw them then – and plenty of others I have come to appreciate over these years), and I certainly could live a Gospel life to the full. Being a perfectionist, I have had to learn that it is OK, and often best, for things to be good enough. That has taken some years! The essential thing is to be ready to give it all you've got – and, for St Benedict, never to give up!

Not being able to make much sense of what was going on, I remember talking about the vocation thing with a good college friend of mine. He thought you can fall in love with God rather as you fall in love with another person. I was encouraged by the way he was so relaxed about celibacy (for someone else), but I also remember feeling it was not quite like that. Friends are at least 'there'; you get something back from them; there is the fun of doing things together, and trivial things too. For me God wasn't there in that kind of way at all, and prayer seemed dead serious. I must say I did not find any of that at all easy – I did not then see how God seems to enjoy little ironies, or how we can find him in a shared delight in small things. On the other hand it dawned on me that among the most human beings I knew then were so many Catholic priests whose warmth, humour, interest in people, education and sensitivity were infectious. However real the surrender, it was certainly not all loss; there was a real blessing too. There were so many people I met over those confused and confusing years who, by their sheer humanity, made Christ's warmth and friendship real. For me it was an encouragement, an invitation and a challenge to respond to his love.

So the crunch eventually came with the Appointments Committee. You can't fall in love with a monastery but there was something like that going on. I knew that the most important thing in my life was God; I had found him at Downside, and that was where I would have to start seeking him, whichever path I was eventually going to be called to follow. I certainly hoped that would be as a monk, though I knew I could not be certain of that. But it was a decision I came to with a wonderful sense of freedom flowing from it. It was presumably what St Augustine meant by saying 'Love and do what you will.' I have always loved monastic life. Even when the going has been very hard indeed, and I have doubted my own powers of survival; but I have never stopped wanting to be a monk.

FIRST STEPS

It was not difficult at first. I arrived at Downside in January 1980 and, as postulant and novice, I think was as happy as I had ever been, for which, of course, much is due to the novice master and those in the novitiate at the time. I felt I had fallen into what I really wanted to live, and I could not imagine things better, though I badly missed seeing my family. This was particularly painful at Christmas and remained so for years. And I lost touch with nearly all my school and university friends, but this seemed to be much less significant then than nowadays when, thanks to modern technology, keeping in constant touch with that kind of network has become, I think, a bit of a neurosis.

Downside gave me just what I realized in Oxford I wanted: a stable pattern of Christian life, dedicated to the service and love of God whom I was able to find in the community around me, besides the extended community of those lay-people who work at Downside (although for a novice, contact with people outside the community was very restricted indeed). It was a balanced life, combining study and prayer with work inside the house (lots of cleaning) and in the gardens. The Divine Office at that time had been reduced to an austere skeleton of psalmody and scripture. But although it lacked the shape and colour provided by the monastic tradition of liturgical prayer, it was undoubtedly the common form of prayer with which the community identified at that time, and celebrating it day in, day out, I could feel myself becoming immersed in the deep life of the community. On the other hand, the Mass, celebrated then entirely in Latin and sung entirely with plainchant, really was the liturgical high point. It was celebrated after breakfast too (at a time when monks might have been expected to be getting about their ordinary work and teaching) as the top priority in the working life of the monastery.

Solitude loomed large. The strangest thing to hit me on the first day was something I knew all about, but had never really thought about as part of a way of life: the strict silence. This was observed from after Compline until after breakfast, for nearly eleven hours; and then there was a list of times and places of silence, which seemed to cover much of the rest of the day, except when we were working in the gardens in the afternoon or at recreation, about half-an-hour after lunch and supper. In the event this silence came to be very important to me, and although there were really tough times when I felt lonely, it was not long before I realized how important it was to learn to be on my own, and to have time and space to get to know myself from inside, with all that that began to disclose to me. It opened up a completely unsuspected interior space for God. Central to this were the two half-hours of silent personal prayer in our daily routine, traditionally known as Mental Prayer, which we were told were something of a Downside speciality. I think it was the most enriching thing about monastic life, and I am sure it is what has made me happiest at Downside; what I did not bargain for was the time it would take to grow into this new form of life.

CHALLENGES

The real problems began soon after Simple Profession, once I had made my initial commitment for three years, and they got worse and worse. It was really as easy as anything for me to be totally deferential; it was something I had had a lot of practice in over the first year and a half. I found it much harder working with others, especially when I had to give a lead to others in the novitiate whose dispositions were different from my own. Downside was then a community of over 40 monks, including some very strong personalities among the older members, as well as an entire cadre, as it seemed, of monks responsible for the school and administration. These monks and the presence of several others in the community who had themselves been in the school, who all seemed completely at ease with the social world of boarding school education and all that went with it, left me feeling rather out of place and unsure of myself. There was clearly a kind of 'belonging' to the community that was much harder to acquire than ordinary monastic observance and went deeper than it.

It felt like a godsend then, after that first year of temporary vows, to be sent to St Benet's Hall, Oxford, to begin my theological formation. Here there was a much smaller community of students. The relative informality of such a group and the common sense of purpose of a House of Studies contrasted with the much larger scale and formality of things at Downside, much to my relief. It was not without its own community tensions, but here I found what I had missed at Downside, a group of young monks, including shorter term visitors, who were able to share their ideals and the problems, common to most junior monastics, of trying to engage with the real situations and histories of our respective monasteries.

It was certainly here that I began to appreciate the appeal of community life at a much more personal level. Now I can see that it is quite common to have a sense of not really fitting in or belonging to a community at more than surface level. It takes a long time to develop what St Benedict seems to be describing in the eighth degree of

131

humility where the monk is content to live by the common rule of the monastery and the example of his seniors without feeling it is just a one-sided act of surrender to someone else's status quo. In the early 1980s I think that well-established, large but a little top-heavy communities were still able to conduct a style of monastic life whose assumptions and expectations of community life were increasingly at odds with the idealism and hopes of the generation of younger people entering monastic life (or seeking to do so); it was easy to overlook this where people were used to working hard, especially in the service of the Church and education. In my case, without any experience of anything better, it brought out rather painfully a longstanding sense of loneliness, a personal neediness from my earlier life I simply did not know what to do with.

So I am very grateful for the friendships that I began to discover then. But there was still a long way to go. Things became even more difficult for me when I returned from Oxford to make my Solemn Profession and to begin to work in the school. Here I suddenly found myself trying to teach children whose interests were quite different from my own. For them, godliness and good learning belonged in two completely different worlds, if either concept meant much to them at all. It took me years to realize (and it was a 14-year-old boy who eventually explained it to me!) that they looked on learning as a kind of game with the teacher, who had to win it, even though the pupils had the considerable advantage, it seemed, of being able to make (nearly) all the rules. At the time, able to function less and less even at a basic level of community life, I wondered simply if I would be able to survive.

The community was very supportive, and I was presumably unable to show much appreciation for the kindness shown in many ways, because I simply could not understand what was going on: it just felt as if I were falling to pieces. However, the abbot got me to see the doctor who put me in touch with a counsellor who really did help me at least begin to address the classroom problems; and even more so, others that arose four years down the line after my return from Rome. Someone once said that the path to God is a kind of spiral coil, continually dipping down into the same kind of difficulties in our shadow self, always a little bit deeper, which actually makes the next phase of growth possible. It is easy to label my problem as inability to be assertive due to a lack of self-esteem. It was a very different matter learning to deal with it. And there was more to it. I had just made my Solemn Profession; monastic life was what I really wanted, and which I was sure at one level brought the best out of me. But now I can see that I still needed to make that life-long commitment fully part of myself, and the school problems only exacerbated the sense I had of not really fitting in.

FINDING THE WAY FORWARD

Another anxiety had been the question of completing my theological studies, about which there had been a lot of uncertainty, but where things had finally resolved in favour of my going to Rome to study Patristics, the theology of the early Christian writers. I cannot exaggerate the importance for me personally of the three years I spent there (1986–89). Apart from the studies, which I loved, and the immediacy of the experience of worldwide Catholicism in all its extraordinary complexity that Rome provides, not least in terms of the world-wide and ecumenical dimensions of monastic life – the chaos, noise and pollution of Rome was a spice in the whole thing. It was a time that completely changed my life, a rebirth.

Three things were crucially important. First, I had the time and space to listen to a lot of the stuff that had been churning around in me and which had made things so difficult. I remember the time spent just sitting in front of the crucifix in the church, a crucifix like the famous one of St Francis that somehow spoke of new life flowing from the cross. Sitting there, I found a safe space in which to let things just come to the surface and just be there. Looking at Jesus helped me learn to accept, to love through the self-hatred I realized lurked so much in the shadows; and to begin to let go of a past I saw I could grow out of. That was the most elusive part. It is so like forgiveness, not because anyone is to blame – if anything, it was more a question of forgiving myself – but because it has its own way of making room for grace to change things. I began to see how deeply a sense of self-pity insinuates itself into our lives, and how unconsciously we organize our lives around an implicit conception of ourselves as a victim. There is a strong instinct in lots of people to prefer death to life. The second big shift flowed from this when I woke up to the fact that in Rome I could really do pretty much what I wanted; but that this gave me the chance to take responsibility for being a monk – it is too easy to use our vocation as permission to avoid responsibility (and play the victim again). However successfully or not, I realized I had to cultivate a monastic conscience if I was going to thrive. The third thing was again the extraordinary chance to share so much with monastic confrères in Sant'Anselmo and to build up a sense of community with really strong human bonds.

This changed my whole outlook on myself and on monastic life. It was tremendously liberating. So much so that I was extremely nervous about coming back home. I remember saying to the abbot (unfairly, I admit, but that is how it felt) how Rome had changed me, and I was not going to let Downside change me back! But, at the same time, I knew I wanted to give myself unreservedly to Downside at last; I was just unsure how it would all work out. In addition, it was hard letting go of Rome. I badly missed the friends I had made there. It took about a year, I think, to reintegrate myself. Life in a regular monastery just is less exciting; there was less going on and there was less space and time that I could make my own now that I was fully engaged in the working life of the community. But the miracle was that whereas I had left for Rome feeling a total failure at Downside and wondering whether I would ever be able to get back, here I was (to my astonishment) finding work in the school more or less manageable and enormously rewarding, and with nerves left for other responsibilities too. And for the first time really feeling that I could make friends with others in the community, or friendships deep enough to thrive.

One of the biggest interior milestones on my journey was passed before I ever left Rome. It was a few months after that conversation with the abbot. I was coming back in a bumpy Roman bus from Cerveteri with a monastic friend, driving like a whirlwind out of a thunderstorm that had suddenly concluded an archaeological picnic in the Etruscan cemetery. Lying in the sun under the fragrant pine trees there, lives in my mind as an almost ecstatic moment of utter peace; then, running soaked by the rain for that idiotic bus, one of those ridiculous moments that makes life human. And approaching the urban sprawl of Rome again brought us both back to earth and to the impending returns we both had to make to our respective monasteries.

We had shared a lot of our hopes and anxieties of monastic life over the years we had been together at Sant' Anselmo, and this time I began to unburden myself of my fears about going back to Downside. As far as I was

135

concerned I was just letting off steam as so many junior monks at Rome tended to do. But then it suddenly became serious. 'Well, why don't you just leave?' he asked. 'I can't do that . . . I can't possibly do that', trotting out the reasons I always had for not being able to 'just leave'. Always the question, 'But why not just leave?' In an extraordinary way he was forcing me to take responsibility for my own life and the commitments I had made to my brethren for better and for worse. I can only think he must have got very fed up with my moaning. He would not accept the fact that I had already made my Solemn Profession: lots of people leave after Solemn Profession. He would not accept the unspoken sense of injured pride and loss of face at just walking out: lots of people manage it very successfully. And suddenly I found myself saying 'I don't want to.' Again, 'Why not?' And suddenly I woke up to the fact that through all the anguish, it was the community that had given me the chance to live the only life I wanted to live. As with an old friend, I suddenly woke up to the power of a love I had for Downside in spite of (or because of) everything else.

TAKING STOCK

In the middle of my life's journey, I know there remains much that is still working itself out, but I have to say that I do feel that, for the time being at least, the path is rather easier to follow. Over the 17 years since coming back, the main thing is how glad I am to have been able to get stuck into things and live out with and for others something of what has been most precious to me in my innermost self. I am conscious of the huge privilege it has been to help other young men at the outset of their monastic lives, both as novice master and in other less formal ways. For seven years I was School Chaplain, a job I was certain was totally beyond me, and although I had been teaching happily enough for a few years after my return from Rome, I felt the panic again that had overwhelmed me in first years in the school. But it was a job where I feel I did make a difference, and when I handed the job on three years ago to return to the novitiate as novice master, and subsequently in serving as Prior, I can only say they were seven wonderfully rich years of monastic life, including moments of happiness I had hardly dreamt of.

It is hard to describe the sense of privilege it is to work as closely as possible in a school like ours with both staff and pupils in such a precious sphere as people's hearts and souls. One moment that brought it home to me was when I had been asked to look after the Lead Inspector on the night before the start of a School Inspection. After an enjoyable conversation, suddenly he asked me what, in my work as chaplain, were my criteria for success? I had never asked myself the question – perhaps I should have done – but what *does* count as success for a chaplain? The number of confirmations? Or conversions? The volume of hymn singing? I ventured it was something we only find out in heaven. Evidently that was not a satisfactory answer. But it left me thinking, how does one measure a smile or the wisdom a young person has acquired in addressing the challenges of life outside school, or his generosity of heart towards his fellows? And yet it is in nourishing this kind of faith, hope and love among the pupils and staff that I have found them growing in myself a bit, together with the joy that comes with growth in Christian life.

And besides the school, I found great pleasure in trying to share some of the fruits of my experience of monastic life with people in parishes, as well as giving talks and retreats. I think the peculiar circumstances of the origins of English Benedictine monasticism, where the pressing needs of supporting persecuted Catholics in this country after the Reformation not only called for martyrs among my brethren but also for pastors, have given us an incredible blessing in teaching us to seek out ways of using our monastic life to serve the Church through the priesthood.

It has helped me appreciate more clearly what I had always admired in the ideal of godliness and good learning I had assimilated at school: the Incarnation of Christ models the way that human culture is made for God to disclose himself to us in revelation, and that the Gospel of Christ always summons us to make our culture a medium in which it can be communicated. For me, education is about helping young people grow in faith and understanding of the mystery of God. A school needs to be a place where people learn to be contemplatives, and at its heart must always be a community of worship. Monasteries make for very good schools! But I have also come to appreciate more clearly how the Incarnation finds its completion in the mystery of Redemption; and education always needs to lead people beyond understanding to a living out of faith for the salvation of others. It must be a call to service and sacrifice. Monasteries should be schools of vocation.

DREAMS AND VISIONS

It is not so hard to look back and see the story taking shape. What its end will be is obviously beyond anyone's telling now. But it makes me try to take stock of how I see things from where I have arrived. I think the challenge at the moment is fidelity to the commitment to seek God before all else, as well as fidelity to my own community, and keeping that commitment alive. Perhaps I am more conscious now, in the middle of the journey, of how easy it is to settle for less than the fullness of life that the Gospel is all about and which St Benedict seems to think vocation is all about when he depicts God, in the Prologue to the *Rule*, asking people 'if anyone longs for life and to see good days' (*RB*, Prologue, 15). It is easy to lose the zest and idealism of the outset of the monastic path and just make do with being busy; especially doing things we can say are pastoral work, part of our service of the Church. Not that I still try to run up stairs two at a time. But I do think that it is dangerous to lose sight of the vision, just because there are so many more immediate responsibilities to occupy the mind. One of the signs of the end times is that young men will see visions, and old men will dream dreams (cf. Joel 2.28).Young people naturally look ahead and are eager to get there; an older generation, which has absorbed the memory and unconscious life of the community, will be slower, more cautious, mindful of the past and possibly haunted by it. People in mid-life somehow have to be a bit of both. Both are needed too: to look ahead wisely we need to remember and re-member the past.

I think many monks and nuns find that they are perfectionists. Monastic life, after all, speaks to that kind of instinct which is idealistic, ambitious and dedicated. But there is the shadow side to it, the '-ism'. We can expect the earth of everyone else, and are quick to write ourselves off as no good, because we don't come up to those standards either; and/or other people's failure to measure up makes us feel we don't need to bother either, or cross because we cannot be as casual as others seem to be. I can certainly find myself somewhere in the middle of all that. Besides the Jesus Prayer, two mantras have come to be very important: one bears on others, 'it takes all sorts' – people just are very different, and things are much the better for it; the other relates to my own inertia (both with starting and with finishing things), 'just do it'. It has taken a bit of time, too, to learn to 'make do' and 'make good' – both of which can

139

be heard as a call to acceptance, but also a challenge – and also that things can be 'good enough' and that that is all right, at least provisionally. For it seems to me to spell the end of monastic life if we throw away our sense of idealism; the challenge we have is to engage thoroughly with the imperfect stuff of human life and the legacy of a community's half-lived story in order to reach our supernatural goal, which will always be a rather tight fit for our natural lives.

SEASONS OF THE SPIRIT

Perhaps the lesson that I have gradually learnt is the importance of patience, of knowing that often the only thing we can do is put ourselves and others in the way of grace, and create a kind of hopeful space where people can let God work. For me a sense of humour is vital here to keep our perspective on things open for God to surprise us. Laughter and smiling seem to me such precious gifts; not as a forced thing, but rather the ability always to find the possibility or the hope of a smile. Faith and hope seem to go so closely together; as the Letter to the Hebrews puts it (11.1): 'Faith is the substance of things hoped for.' Together they enable love. But the gift of faith seems to be born out of an experience of covenant, a recognition of God's enduring faithfulness to us. And as our lives proceed, this work is typically a redemptive work, which is won, sometimes only very slowly, through learning to forgive the past and see God's hand in it. The point though is to respect the seasons of the Spirit, and that winter, the season for recounting the past, has its part to play in the advent of spring. Growth in the spirit always comes, not by expanding, but by dying and rising.

Writing this story reminds me of a wonderful piece of advice I was given from the Anglican priest who wrote to me when I shared with him my anxiety about becoming a Catholic, and needing to know I was doing the right thing. He showed me I was asking the wrong question: I could never have the certainty of knowing I was doing the right thing; but there was a different kind of certainty, a certainty of faith. The only thing that mattered was to be guided by the Holy Spirit; and we can only judge that in terms of faith by trying to live the life of the Spirit and see what kind of fruit it bore in terms of 'love, joy, peace, patience, kindness, goodness, faithfulness, gentleness and self-control' (Gal. 5.22). That journey, I have to admit, has still a long way to go.

Straight Writing on Crooked Lines

Agnes Wilkins

The last thing I wanted to do with my life was to become a nun. I was educated by nuns at primary school, secondary school, and the College of Education I attended to train as a teacher, so took these rather unusual beings very much for granted; they were just part of my life. But for all that, they remained decidedly 'different'. I suppose I thought they were somehow not fully human; certainly I had no curiosity about their way of life, nor the slightest inclination to join them. Perhaps that is not quite true: when I was 12 or 13, and a pupil at the local convent grammar school, I did feel a pull towards the religious life, but I grew out of it and dismissed all such ideas from my mind. Of course, I knew nothing about the distinction between apostolic religious sisters (who teach or have some active work) and 'contemplatives' who usually live a life devoted to prayer within the enclosure of the monastery. I had not even heard of the monastic life – there were no monks or nuns in my area.

This, then, is the story of my vocation, of how I changed from total indifference, bordering on aversion, to embracing the monastic form of religious life wholeheartedly, and how, despite the 'crooked lines' of my life, God has written his name clearly over it all, and claimed me for himself. And I discovered, to my surprise, that monastic life is the most human life you can live. What do I mean by that? I believe there is a 'monastic archetype', that is to say, each of us (whether we are aware of it or not) married or single, holy or unholy, rich or poor, has a little bit of the monk or nun inside us – a part of ourselves accessible to God alone. And so, in a sense, everyone's journey has a touch of the monastic about it. The vowed monastic way of life gives outward expression to this in the fullest manner possible, and I have discovered that in following my Benedictine vocation, I have become fully alive as a human being.

A YORKSHIRE CHILDHOOD

There was nothing in my early years that would suggest that I was destined for the religious life. I am a 'cradle Catholic', nurtured from my earliest years in a religious, though not at all pious, environment; in fact, quite the opposite. I was born in Scarborough on the north-east coast of Yorkshire in Holy Week of 1944, and I would say the first ten years or so of my childhood were carefree and secure. I had two younger brothers and a sister, and I remember happy occasions when our mother would take us to play on the beach, or our father would take us on long cycle rides. I was quite big for my age and something of a tomboy, even a bully at times. My long-suffering mother would occasionally have to bear the brunt of my unruly behaviour when neighbours complained about me. However, she was a wonderful mother, and I am convinced I owe my religious vocation, after God's call, to her prayers. She herself had entered the religious life with the Sisters of Mercy in her youth, but left, I believe because she felt so strongly that she

143

wanted to have a family. But she never lost her love of the religious life and hoped it would come out in her children. Before all else, she would have liked a son who was a priest, but unfortunately neither of my brothers obliged her on that score. Nevertheless, it was quite good enough for her that I should be a nun, though she never once suggested it to me, or exerted pressure on any of us as to the way our futures should develop. It was a great blessing to feel so unconditionally loved, and free to be one's self. She herself never wavered in her simple, heartfelt piety, yet she was ahead of her time in her ecumenical outreach. Ministers of the local Protestant churches would gather regularly in our house for Bible study. But the real core of her life was attendance at the daily Eucharist. Wild horses could not keep her away from it, whatever the weather or her state of health. I think over the years of my childhood I imbibed my faith from her, much more than from anything I learned at school.

My school years at the local Catholic primary school were on the whole contented. My bullying tendencies were still evident and I would be pulled up from time to time for fighting in the playground. But apart from that, I got on well with my teachers, and learned diligently, usually coming somewhere towards the top of the class at the end of the school year. Mine was just a typical Catholic education of the time. Things started to go wrong when I was about 13 or 14 years of age, and this largely owing to the break-up of my parents' marriage. My father, who was a few years younger than my mother, was also a cradle Catholic, but not a very fervent one. He was brought up with a younger brother in Sheffield, West Yorkshire, but their mother died when they were quite young. My father was treated unfairly in that, as money was short, only one of the boys could go to university, and the younger, my father's brother, was the chosen one. I think he always resented this and it was probably in some way the cause of the breakdown of his marriage. In a way my own life followed a similar pattern, in that I too was unable to study for a degree on leaving school, and similarly felt in later life that I had missed out on something. Here in the monastery we have a good library and scope to study privately, but one of the best things that happened to me was to be allowed to take a degree in Catholic Theology by distance learning at the Maryvale Institute in Birmingham. It was tough fitting in such intensive studies with my monastic duties; and long drawn out – it went on for five years – but I never tired of it, and feel enormously enriched. It somehow made me feel more a whole person. Study as well as *lectio divina*, that is, quiet, meditative reading, form an important part of our life, since God has given us minds as well as hearts and spirits to be used in his service.

To return to my father. He was responsible, as Clerk of Works, for various local building projects and also taught a night class. Unfortunately, this did not satisfy him and he wanted to have the university education he had missed in his youth. My mother, generous as ever, let him go to live in Manchester for four years, where he studied at the university as a mature student. This involved great hardship for my mother, who was left to bring up four young children virtually on her own, with much reduced funds. My father obtained a grant but it did not compare with his former earnings. I'm not quite sure how my mother managed financially during these years. Naturally, she was hoping for a better life for all of us when my father finished his studies, but it was not to be. He seemed to change during this study period and grew apart from my mother and the family. His visits home were stressful; arguments easily sprang up between my parents and I was always glad when he had gone. Inevitably, I suppose, he found someone else and would spend much of his holiday periods on the continent where his 'new love' resided. These were very hard times for all of us. My character changed quite a lot. From being outgoing and self-confident, I became shy, introspective, at times even morose. If my father had gone away completely it might have been better, but he tried to live a double life, sometimes at home, sometimes abroad, and to pretend that all was well. I seem to have inherited not a little of his questioning, argumentative character, and when he was at home we would have heated debates about religion, which would upset my mother because her faith was so simple and sure. Mine questioned everything, and she may have thought I was losing it. In this she was probably right.

FALLING AWAY ...

I don't remember exactly what made me lapse from the faith. It was a gradual process during my teenage years, although I always went to Mass on Sundays as long as I lived at home. I know one thing that bothered me (it still does) was the Church's doctrine of hell as a place of eternal punishment. Today I am attracted to the 'heresy' of *apokatastasis*, which claims that hell is not forever and that, finally, all will be saved. I was very happy to discover a book by the eminent theologian Hans Urs von Balthasar called *Dare we Hope that All may be Saved?*[1] He risked his reputation at the end of his life with the writing of this book, so I feel I am in good company.

In my teenage years, because of troubles at home, my school work deteriorated. I see now what was obscure at the time: that I was suffering because my parents were splitting up. I longed to draw them back to each other, but it was totally beyond my ability to do so, and I sank into depression. I could not understand why I felt so miserable. I did not associate it with the situation with my parents at all; it was just bewildering. I failed my GCE exams miserably. I sat for eight or nine subjects and passed only three. Although I re-sat and passed three of them in the autumn, I did not continue with 'A'-level studies. My mother was worried about me and took me to the doctor, who referred me to a psychiatrist at the local hospital. I don't remember much about it or how long it went on, but it helped me to make the difficult decision to leave school. This was definitely one of the 'crooked lines' of my life. It was probably a wrong decision, but God, in his own way, has turned it to my good.

I worked in a bread and cake shop for a while, then took a secretarial course for a year at the local technical college, after which I obtained an office job in a department store. My father was very disappointed in me for leaving school since he wanted me to 'achieve' by succeeding academically and going to university; something I too desired but did not feel I could attain at the time. I do not think it occurred to him that he may have been partly responsible for this situation. My relationship with him grew worse and had the effect of giving me a negative attitude to men in general. I had no desire to get married or to have children and did not have a 'normal' adolescence, in that I socialized very little, and did not have much fun. I had one very faithful school friend and we spent a lot of time together just talking at her house or mine, or going for walks. I did have one boyfriend when I was about 16, the son of a friend of my mother's and whose parents were divorced. He used to come to Scarborough occasionally to see his mother. Those encounters were real moments of light and joy, but few and far between, and as we became older the relationship just petered out.

147

Although my commitment to the institutional Church was very weak at this time, God was reaching out to me in other ways, for instance during the long solitary walks I used to love to take by the sea. There is something fascinating about the sea: its endless horizon is a symbol of eternity and a strong reminder of the 'other shore'. How I missed it (and still do) when I had to move inland. The sea is always in motion, never the same two days running: sometimes a silver sheen of peacefulness, very quiet, while at other times it unleashes wild forces that leave you in awe of nature's power. It is easy to sense a 'divine presence' when alone amid nature's grandeur, and I learned to respond in prayer to this awesome 'presence'. Sometimes I would end my walks sitting at the back of St Peter's church where I was baptized and made my first confession and communion. I often felt very weak and wounded because of the situation at home, but somehow sensed some solace in the dark gloom of the church, and the proximity of the living presence of the Lord.

THE RETURN

When I was 19 I began to feel the need to break out of what had become a very narrow existence. The prospect of leaving home filled me with anxiety but I knew I had to do it if I was to grow as a person. And so I found myself heading for the city of Bradford in industrial West Yorkshire – not a very prepossessing place but it did provide plenty of secretarial work. Although this was not work I would have chosen to do nor did I enjoy it very much, it was good to be independent and to learn to stand on my own two feet. I wanted to improve my lot, however, and obtain more satisfying work, and so I applied to Endsleigh College of Education in Hull which was run by the Sisters of Mercy.

(In fact it adjoined the very convent where my mother had been a novice.) I do not know whether they were favourably disposed towards me because of that, but I was accepted despite having no 'A'-level qualifications.

My outward practice of the faith was fairly weak by this time, now that my mother could not see whether I went to Mass or not. However I was still nominally a Catholic and never lost my faith in God. Nor did he ever stop reaching out to me, despite my feeble response. Ironically, it was not until I went to a Catholic college where I could seriously question aspects of my faith that I was able to find my way back to the institutional Church. I remember while I was at college deliberately missing Mass for quite a time because I did not want to go just because I was afraid of committing a mortal sin, which I had been taught would deprive the soul completely of grace. There had to be something more to religion than simply being good enough to be in a 'state of grace'. I wanted to experience what it was like to be in the state I feared (it used to be considered a 'mortal sin' to miss Mass on Sundays). Would I still be able to have some form of communication with God or would all that be cut off? All I remember is that nothing dreadful happened to me and I continued for quite a while not going to Mass, but having gone down that road, a real indifference set in, at least for the time being. My way back came in a rather unexpected way.

But this is to run ahead of the story. To return to my time in Bradford – I continued my usual stay-at-home behaviour and in the evenings mostly sat companionably with my hosts watching television; that is, until they began to urge me to go out sometimes. So, rather against my inclination, I agreed to go to a dance with their daughter who was a few years older than I. That turned out to be quite an eventful dance since I met a Kuwaiti pharmacy student who became a close friend right up until the time I entered the monastery. He was very sociable, outgoing and friendly, and came from a stable family background, a very good foil for my shyness and the insecurity resulting from my own family background. All this was fine except for the fact that he happened to be a Muslim. Mixed marriages across cultures and religions are never easy. Common sense told me it would be best not to go too far down that road. However, at the time I did not want to get married, so I took no notice. Perhaps this was another of my 'crooked lines', but God in his wisdom worked even this to my good, in that it was through this friendship that I received the great blessing of recovering my faith from which later sprang my religious vocation. How could this be so? On the human level I entered a period of real happiness which can only have been good for me. I felt loved and appreciated for myself, and flourished as a person. As mentioned above, because of my poor relationship with my father, I had a prejudicial dislike for men in general (another effect of this poor relationship was that I could not relate to God as Father until I had been in the monastery for some years), and had no great desire to get married and have a family. However, as a direct result of this friendship, I knew I could get married if that should prove to be my vocation, and be quite happy in that state. Even the thought of having children had some appeal.

Somehow it was necessary for me to get to this degree of acceptance before I embarked upon the monastic life in the course of which I would renounce the prospect of marriage for ever. There is not a great deal of merit in taking religious vows if you do not realize what you are giving up by this solemn act of placing in God's hands your whole future. No longer would I be able to run my own affairs, have regular contact with my family, travel and see the world, let alone marry and have children. Of course it is quite possible to follow the monastic way, and no doubt many do, having given themselves wholeheartedly to the Lord from an early age, automatically cutting out exclusive friendships with the opposite sex. But for me it was otherwise, and I doubt that I could have persevered without the stabilizing experience of this friendship. Do I miss any of these things now? Yes I do. At first the initial impetus of my vocation carried me forwards, but after a few years I often wished I had married and had children, or that I was free to travel abroad and see the world, and various other things, but I have discovered that these are the times when I must recommit myself, and follow wholeheartedly the path which the Lord has marked out for me. But deep down, no, I don't regret anything.

THE CALL

To continue my story. When I met this Kuwaiti friend I had already been accepted at Endsleigh College of Education in Hull, so it was not long before I left Bradford. However we corresponded all during the time I was there and met regularly in the holidays. There was a genuine mutual love which was most fulfilling, but gradually the Lord began to, how shall I say, 'intervene'. I had a vague feeling of unease; I became gradually aware that love on the purely human level, however deep, would never satisfy me. I became aware of another love which transcended the human, and it kept calling me more and more insistently until I had to make a choice. The Lord 'showed' himself to me – not in a visionary sense, but I had a very strong impression of Jesus in his weakness as the Crucified One who had sacrificed himself for love of me, whereas my friend in comparison appeared strong and attractive. I could not help being drawn to the Lord and knew I had to give myself to him

151

exclusively, but it was not yet clear to me what form my life should take.

All this was happening towards the end of my second year at college, and at about the same time the former superior of the nuns I had gone to school with in Scarborough came to talk to the students about the prospect of teaching in Africa. She had a brother who was a White Father (now called Missionaries of Africa) who was working in Uganda, where Catholic teachers were needed at the school run by nuns. I had now returned to the practice of my faith and this idea of missionary work appealed to me very much, so I applied. Then, in the holidays between my second and third year, I spent some time in France, since my special subject was French and I had to do some research for a long essay. It was not really a happy time as I continued to be very aware of the Lord calling me to something – I did not know to what ultimately, and all preparations for a teaching career were losing their grip on me. I had not received a reply to my letter applying for a post in Uganda (I discovered later that one had been sent but never reached me), and remember quite clearly, one day towards the end of my stay in France, sitting quietly in the back of a car after a day out, and thinking what to do with my life, wondering why I had not received a reply to my application to teach in Uganda, when it suddenly dawned on me that the Lord wanted me to be a nun. It seems, in retrospect, a rather illogical conclusion to have drawn, but it was very real and filled me with light and happiness. The way forward seemed clear at last.

Any religious community would have done for me at that moment; I hardly knew about the distinction between the apostolic and contemplative orders, nor did it matter. I was led to Stanbrook when, quite by chance, I came across a copy of *In a Great Tradition*,[2] which describes the history of

152

the community from its foundation in Cambrai, Flanders, during penal times, almost to the present, in the college library at the beginning of my final year. I visited Stanbrook Abbey in the Christmas holidays and Abbess Elizabeth Sumner gave me a warm welcome. She considered I was a good age to enter – I was 22: too young, I think, and still fairly immature. I have often thought it would have been better to have taught for a time, or even to have gone to Africa for a few years, but God calls us when he calls us and his time is best. In any case I could not have done all those things; it was difficult enough concentrating on my third year of studies. I just wanted to give myself to the Lord, enter the monastery as soon as possible, and get on with it.

STANBROOK

I spent my final few weeks at home in the summer of 1967 and left in early September. The goodbye to my family at Scarborough railway station was almost casual, and I don't think any of them expected me to stay for long. I certainly did not really appreciate what a big step I was taking. My Kuwaiti friend met me at Worcester and drove me by car to Stanbrook. I said a brief goodbye at the bottom of the drive and walked to the monastery door alone carrying my luggage. I look back on this deeply symbolic moment with great affection and wistfulness. It was the moment I turned my back on marriage and 'the world' forever, but at the time it was very ordinary; I thought it would not 'look right' knocking at the front door with him at my side – especially as I was late!

How to describe in this short space nearly 40 years of monastic life? It is a life which is very difficult to describe in words. There are several fundamentals common to all Benedictines, such as the liturgy, personal prayer, asceticism, *lectio divina*, study, community life, manual labour; but within that framework the journey of each one is unique, just as all the events in a person's life leading up to entrance into the monastery are unique. We are given a framework within which we pursue our individual way to God, but the essence of that 'framework' is people – not people we would necessarily have chosen to live with, but chosen for us by God – and together we have embarked upon something much greater than we bargained for when we entered. Speaking for myself, I realize now I had very little idea of what I was entering into, and had I known I would probably have fled away in alarm.

LITURGY 24/7/365

Possibly the biggest surprise when I first entered was the impact and importance of the liturgy. Of course I knew beforehand that quite a lot of singing went on in the choir; in fact it was the haunting quality of sung Vespers, the monastery's evening prayer, when I made my first visit, that drew me to this particular monastery, but I was not prepared for the fact that the liturgy would give a whole new dimension to life. What do I mean? Well, liturgical time, I discovered, is not quite the same as secular time. I had been used to thinking of time as it related to college terms and holiday time, with Sunday Mass merely a liturgical punctuation, soon forgotten as one went on to other things. In the monastery, however, one actually lived the liturgy 24/7/365. Even meals were governed by it. So on feast days, for instance, according to the degree of their solemnity, we could expect fairly lavish fare, whereas every day in Lent the food, though normally sufficient in quantity, was boring in the extreme. Most nights I remember having a boiled egg, all on its own (to be joined later by bread and jam), rolling around on a steel plate. But I found that the Eucharist was the heart of the daily liturgy and also, I would say, of the whole of monastic life.

I soon discovered that we were a sort of micro-Church, representing and encapsulating the whole of the universal Church, praying unceasingly for her needs and those beyond her physical boundaries, in fact for the whole world. Having sung Mass every day was a great joy. The same cannot be said for the Divine Office, however. When I entered, the Vatican II liturgical reforms were just beginning to take effect and we were in the process of changing over from huge black volumes of the Latin office – four needed throughout the year – to a complete reshaping of the Office in English. My monastery, I now appreciate, was a pioneer in this area, but it was no fun for a newcomer having to cope with endless bits of paper with new compositions (usually nowhere to be found next time you needed them), as we gradually made the transition, creating our new English Office as we went along. No, it was not easy getting used to this and it tried my patience considerably. Also difficult was the fact that I had to learn to take an active part in the liturgy. My shyness about singing solo in public (I was made a chantress fairly early on) took a long time to overcome. Those difficulties apart, I learned to live the liturgy as the rock and foundation of daily life. I loved Sundays especially when I could dwell for the whole day on the Resurrection, and the other feast days were like oases in a life which could sometimes feel like a long trek through the desert. Liturgical time is somehow more real than secular time: we are living the Christian mysteries, the basic realities of our faith, going deeper into them each year like a corkscrew going into a bottle of wine, as my novice mistress used to say. Amazingly, this is an aspect of the life which never loses its impact over time – that particular wine bottle has infinite depths.

155

THE CHALLENGE OF PRAYER

Another big challenge on entering the monastery is that one has to live a serious life of personal prayer apart from the Divine Office. Two half-hour periods are allotted each day which the novice dutifully has to fulfil in church. One has to confront the darkness within, and in the process, oneself. My own call to a life of prayer began, as I have described, before I entered the monastery. Early in my novitiate I came across the poem '*Desiderium Indesideratum*' by Francis Thompson which summed up for me the essence of that call as it came to me then and continues to do so. It was about a certain 'pull' that would not, and still will not, let me settle in anything less than God himself. It began as follows:

O gain that lurk'st ungainèd in all gain!
O love we just fall short of in all love!
O height that in all heights art still above!
O beauty that dost leave all beauty pain!
Thou unpossessed that mak'st possession vain ...[3]

At first it was not a happy experience to pray, and had it not been built into the daily timetable, it would have been tempting to give up altogether. Fortunately, one has a guide in the novice mistress to lead one through the early pitfalls. I was told that the prayer which sustained me before entering, and got me over the threshold, so to speak, was going to change. It is as if, having succeeded in enticing you into the monastery, the Lord suddenly disappears. This, as all the manuals on prayer tell us, is St John of the Cross' 'night of sense', in which one has to learn to love God for himself alone, not for any of his gifts. Inevitably, I felt a deep sense of abandonment and loneliness, and in words from another poem of Francis Thompson, would cry out inwardly, 'This

love is crueller than the other love ...'⁴ Union with God
seemed unattainable, mysterious, intangible. Yet I knew I
had embarked on a real love affair. It is a process of gradual
acceptance, saying 'yes' to God, not only in prayer, but in
every detail of daily life. It all seems a bit dislocated at the
beginning, but gradually prayer becomes the cement that
holds everything together.

Towards the end of my novitiate I came across another
poem, this time by Alice Meynell, called 'The Poet to his
Childhood'. The poet speaks of the loneliness of her
vocation, how she had not realized when she set off, full of
enthusiasm in her youth, how difficult it was going to be. It
seemed to apply to my own vocation: I set off enthusiastically but with very little idea of what the life was about
and the demands it would make on me. As Meynell did, I
learned to look back affectionately at myself as I began, a
child spiritually, and say 'yes' all over again as an adult,
when at least some of the difficulties had become clear.
What follows is a section of the poem:

In my thought I see you stand with a path on either
hand,
Hills that look into the sun, and there a river'd
meadowland.
And your lost voice with the things that it decreed
across me thrills
When you thought, and chose the hills.

If it prove a life of pain, greater have I judged the gain.
With a singing soul for music's sake, I climb and meet
the rain,
And I choose, whilst I am calm, my thought and
labouring to be
unconsoled by sympathy.

But how dared you use me so? For you bring my ripe years low
To your child's whim and a destiny your child-soul could not know.
And that small voice legislating I revolt against, with tears.
　But you mark not, through the years.

And the final verse:

I rebel not, child gone by, but obey you wonderingly,
For you knew not, young rash speaker, all you spoke, and now will I,
With the life, and all the loneliness revealed that you thought fit,
　Sing the Amen, knowing it.[5]

THE MIND HAS MOUNTAINS

It is true there has been a lot of loneliness – to the extent that I have sometimes wondered whether God was calling me to be a hermit, but I know that way of life is not for me, although I have much sympathy for it and anyone who tries to live it. I know now my limitations and that I am not strong enough; I need the support of a community. Nevertheless we all have to live solitude to some degree in community. Is it not part and parcel of being human? We are born alone and we die alone. It has a kind of archetypal quality which monastic life highlights. Moreover, it is an illusion to think that either marriage or close personal friendships whether inside or outside the monastery would take away such feelings. We all have to discover, sooner or later, that there is a part of us which is always alone – a sacred inner core to which God alone has access. For myself,

I have discovered the key thing to hang on to through everything is a very strong attachment to the person of Jesus Christ. The ultimate aim should be to say with St Paul, 'It is no longer I who live, but Christ who lives in me' (Gal. 2.20). Then all other relationships fall into place. I am not there yet; the Lord is sometimes present for me, at other times – even long times – seemingly absent, but he always calls me beyond myself, asking me to trust him when I feel my weakness and unable to live this life by my own strength. Thus I try to strike a balance between my own solitude and community life, a challenge we all have to face.

So have I ever thought of running away because it is all too much, too difficult? Yes I have, fairly frequently, and once I actually did. It was on account of my interest in interreligious dialogue. I wanted to devote my whole life to it in a way that was not possible in the monastery, so I thought I would be justified in leaving to fulfil a call I felt was from God. I soon discovered my mistake. The months, possibly years, before my momentous departure were extremely painful, in fact, one of the most painful times of my life, as I struggled with the demands of monastic obedience and what I felt God might be asking of me. I did not want to leave the monastery at all but felt it was not giving me the scope I needed in this area of interreligious dialogue. It was certainly no simple choice between right and wrong: it seemed that if I stayed in the monastery it could be wrong for me. I became increasingly confused and unhappy. I could not see the way forward at all. I knew I needed to be outside the monastery, at least for a while, to get some clarity and perspective into my thoughts. After much struggle, I decided to leave and, to cut a long story short, found myself on a lonely Welsh hillside one Advent, the darkest time of the year. At first I was happy; I suppose it was the relief of having finally made a decision, combined with the beauty of my surroundings and meeting up with some helpful and sympathetic people. However, I very quickly realized that I had made a big mistake when, returning to the monastery to collect some things, I experienced some powerful emotions.

The antiphons I had sung and the words I had said at my Solemn Profession came flooding back to my mind unbidden and I knew that what had been accomplished in me that day had changed me radically: I would never find 'my place' or 'my vocation' anywhere but in the monastery of my profession. I knew I just had to put on my monastic habit again and return, even if it meant renouncing any involvement in interreligious dialogue. Making such a sudden U-turn was another very stressful experience and my health deteriorated, but after a few months spent in another monastery recovering, I did return to Stanbrook; most fittingly, it was Eastertide. I have never since felt any desire or temptation to leave. Was it difficult coming back? Not at all. It was as if everything were completely new over again, as on the day I first entered. I felt carried by grace, that special help which God gives in time of need, and I was very happy.

THE FREEDOM OF OBEDIENCE

What did I learn from this experience? It has proved to be one of the most formative periods of my life. The first and most significant thing I learned was the fundamental importance of monastic obedience. I had quickly discovered that 'freed' from it, I who had taken a solemn vow of obedience to my superiors, was nothing. Whereas formerly I could never quite go along with what St Benedict says (*RB* 5:12) about monks and nuns actually *desiring* to be under the authority of an abbot or abbess (it was just one of those things you had to put up with), after returning, I discovered that perhaps my deepest desire was to really obey. I am not by nature a very submissive person; quite the contrary, but vowed monastic obedience is our way of expressing love for God, just as in a happy marriage I would imagine each of the partners would want to do the other's will rather than their own. I now felt it would make perfect sense to substitute 'obedience' for 'love' in St Paul's famous hymn to love in 1 Corinthians 13: 'If I have faith enough to move mountains, and am without *obedience*, I am nothing.'

The second thing I learned was that interreligious dialogue, at least for me, is most effectively practised from within the monastery, despite the limitations on travel and opportunities to meet other people. My particular area of interest is in building bridges with Islam, an interest stimulated during a lecture at Burford Priory in the autumn of 2001 (just before 9/11) where the urgency of this debate – tragically confirmed by subsequent events – was stressed. I have since become acquainted with the work of Louis Massignon,[6] a French Islamic scholar who died in 1962. His whole life is fascinating but especially significant is that, having abandoned the Catholicism of his childhood, he was drawn into the study of Islam because of his admiration of a Sufi master, Al-Hallaj (858–922), whom he later made the subject of a doctoral thesis. Massignon subsequently experienced a dramatic conversion while leading an archaeological expedition in Iraq, after which he returned to the Catholicism of his youth. He was convinced that it was chiefly through the intercession of Al-Hallaj, a Muslim saint, that he was led back to Christianity. The value of Massignon for us today is that he has such a strong affinity with Islam from within and so can help us as we struggle to understand the place of this mysterious post-Christian revelation in God's scheme of things.

In the monastery, through living a committed and ever-deepening life of prayer, I have begun to live in the dimension of the All-Embracing Christ, and to desire, as he does, that all humanity should be one in him (cf. Jn 17.21). Moreover, monastics partake in Christ's own prayer both in the liturgy and in personal, silent prayer and so help him to bring about this unity, in heaven ultimately, but also here below, little by little. The life of enclosure does not prevent me from writing articles and attending the occasional meeting. Now enriched by monastic obedience, the 'vocation within a vocation' to interreligious dialogue that I sensed early in my monastic life has worked itself out in ways I could not have foreseen. Although my contribution to this great venture may be modest, when combined with prayer and faith, I believe that God can use it to move mountains.

JOY

I would like to end my story on a note of joy, a joy not to be confused with a superficial, bubbly happiness, but something much deeper. Monastic joy does not even need a smile to express it exteriorly. It is just a deep acceptance of the fact that I am loved and called by God, that he has redeemed me and all humanity through the life, death and resurrection of his Son. He knows how to 'write straight' however crooked we have made the lines, that is, he turns everything to good for those who love him (cf. Rom. 8.28) so that nothing can 'separate us from the love of God in Christ Jesus our Lord' (Rom. 8.39).

NOTES

1. H. U. von Balthasar (1988), *Dare we Hope that All may be Saved?* San Francisco: Ignatius Press.

2. The Benedictines of Stanbrook (1956), *In a Great Tradition*, A Tribute to Dame Laurentia McLachlan, Abbess of Stanbrook. London: John Murray.
3. *The Poems of Francis Thompson* (2001), Brigid M. Boardman (ed.). London/New York (in association with Boston College): Continuum, p. 246.
4. *Ibid.*, from 'Not Even in Dream', p. 218.
5. *The Poems of Alice Meynell* (1947), Centenary edn. London: Hollis & Carter, p. 165.
6. For more information, see my chapter, 'Thomas Merton and Islam' (2006), in A. O'Mahony and P. Bowe OSB (eds), *Catholics in Interreligious Dialogue*. Leominster: Gracewing.

8

'It is Good for us to be Here'

Simon McGurk

What is your opinion? A man had two sons. He went and said to the first, 'My boy, you go and work in the vineyard today'. He answered, 'I will not go', but afterwards thought better of it and went. The man then went and said the same thing to the second who answered, 'Certainly, sir', but did not go. Which of the two did the father's will?

(Mt. 21.28-30, JB)

So, which son am I? Come to think of it, which one are you?

OFF GRAPES

Outwardly, I probably appear to most people as generally good and law-abiding: my parents sent me to a boarding school so I avoided their direct moral scrutiny during the troublesome years, I've kept the right side of my religious superiors, I've only twice been stopped by a policeman, once for speeding and once for not having a bicycle bell; I've kept my nose clean. It would seem to follow from Jesus' teaching that inside I must therefore be full of all evil and wickedness like the Scribes and Pharisees. This may be so but, like them, I am not really aware of it. When I reflect, I find that my tendency is to refuse life's every urging, apart from that of the flesh. I don't want to read the books I should, I don't want to do my physical exercises, I don't want to take my medicine, I too often don't want to pray. I don't want to go to the damned vineyard ... at least not today: I'm off grapes. Yet, despite all this, I seem to have had a happier time than the Scribes and Pharisees. I'll bet they had bicycle bells and look what they did for them.

CREATUREHOOD

My emergence into full creaturehood took place at a nursing home in Rock Ferry, Cheshire, in 1943. We lived for my first 13 years in Bebington, across the River Mersey from Liverpool. My father was a Belfast Catholic of middle-class stock who left Ireland around 1936. He was loveable but fearsome with a proverbial Irish temper. He was utterly religious and dutiful without being oppressive, except on sex and politics; the former you didn't mention, on the latter you didn't disagree. My mother is an English cradle-Catholic. They seemed to have a loving marriage and aunts also abounded to cement any possible cracks. We were four children, an elder sister, Antonia, and a younger sister and brother, Georgina and Ludovic. For us, going to church was completely normal and unquestioned.

Despite my declaration above of appearing to be generally good and law-abiding, I am told that I was particularly naughty in church and for this was promoted, at my father's pleading, to the discipline of the choir, an upper gallery of voluble matrons, caring Irish spinsters and male reed-warblers. I was 8 years old at this crucial juncture of my ecclesiastical elevation, communicated and confirmed, and thus fitted to bestow ecclesiastical havoc from above until, just as suddenly, my father took me off to Mr

Heffernan, a gruff, chain-smoking Irishman who taught me to serve Mass beginning with that single Irish word, *adDeumquilaetificatiuventutemmeum*.

From the nuns of Rock Ferry Convent I was transferred at age 8 to the Christian Brothers at St Anselm's, Birkenhead. Of course, I did not want to go. I had been bullied at the convent and I feared worse at St Anselm's. Yet, at St Anselm's I found peace. Even the bullies seemed to have found other victims. I enjoyed emerging as the class comedian as well as performing well at my studies. But my parents had set their hearts on a boarding school for me. As usual, I did not want to go, especially as my mother fed me with negative psychology based on her own experience so that when I got there it would not seem so awful. Most threatening was the prospect of inescapable luke-warm porridge. It is strange how such incomprehensible parental decisions later become a major influence for the rest of one's life.

SPEARS, SOAP AND THE SLIPPERY SLOPE

So it was off to remotest Derbyshire, to the Benedictine monks at Alderwasley Hall, near Matlock, a world of dens, cowboys and Indians, and Latin. But one day into this idyllic English jungle came the White Fathers from blackest Africa, wearing fezes and bearing spears and other instruments of death, recruiting for future martyrs. Whatever they said was so spiked with Christian self-renunciation that two of us resolved there and then to join up when we were old enough. I have never forgotten how I felt the movement of God at this moment: I just wanted to do the best thing in the world for him whatever it was and whatever the cost. I had seen all the *Punch* cartoons of missionaries standing in pots of boiling oil, but they were

Protestants. If God was what the nuns, the Christian Brothers and the monks said he was, then the best thing in the world was to do whatever he wanted. English Catholicism was still imbued with the cult of oppression and martyrdom even at this time. One just 'bought' martyrdom as the best deal on offer for 'getting you there' quicker, as the early Christians found.

In 1956, at 13, I was transferred to the senior school at Belmont Abbey, Hereford. As the years coursed along one would be asked, 'What are you going to do when you leave?' Somehow, amid all the more obvious worldly answers, I could never think of anything more honest to say than that I wanted to be a priest. Little by little, 'priest' became 'monk', which in those days, at least in the EBC, included being a priest. Basically, the old answer was being redefined in new circumstances. I just wanted to do the best thing in the world. Nothing else made any sense to me and the world made no sense without God. I was already conscious of what I would read many years later in the writings of William of St Thierry: 'As long as I am with you I am present to myself. I am not wholly me when I am not with you.'

Towards the end of my schooling at Belmont I became interested in architecture as a career. They were building Brasilia and I wanted to go there. My friends did not seem to see anything pious or odd about my wanting to be a monk but I realized that it didn't do to mention it too much: architecture made better conversation. Throughout my school days I was quite devout and I had two or three devout and supportive friends. We were not a clique nor particularly 'churchy' but God mattered and we prayed because he was God and not because we wanted something. When we did want something, an exam success or a rugby victory, we prayed like hell but that was different. Woven into this would come the thought of my parents who often

167

seemed remote from the iniquitous refuge of boarding school but whose faith and sense of religious duty were admirable and unflinching. Yet what attracted me to the monastery were just the monks with whom I got on quite well. Their life seemed good, God-centred and dedicated, and to me, a modest sportsman, their brand of muscular Christianity appealed. There was something boyish and human in seeing one's monastic rugby coaches whose Masses one had served in the early morning, laughing and joking in a hot common shower after a game and throwing soap at each other ... and at me. Was soap to be the slippery slope to perfection?

THE FUTURE: CHOICE OR LOTTERY

I left Belmont at 18. The idea of 'monk' had slipped out of heart and mind. I had applied to Manchester University to read architecture and that was to be the future. I just awaited 'A'-level results and a favourable letter. Two weeks before leaving a friend said to me, 'Have you heard? McCarthy's going to be a monk.' McCarthy and I were quite friendly but I had had no idea. Suddenly a huge penny dropped in my conscience: 'That's what I should be doing.' I talked with McCarthy: it was true. I went to see the abbot; he accepted me but said he would call me at home. The long summer holiday was agony as I awaited two conflicting life sentences. Finally, I decided that on whichever day I got whichever call, that I would answer: if it's Monday it's monastery, if it's Tuesday it's architecture, etc. The abbot's letter came on a Wednesday: it was monastery. I was to be there in time for Clothing as a novice on the Feast of St Michael, the patronal feast of Belmont, 29 September 1961. I had probably the shortest postulancy in history, but who needs a postulancy when you've been playing rugby and holding 'illegal' whisky sessions with the same monks only weeks before?

'GOOD FOR US TO BE HERE'

During the first weeks my four fellow novices would talk to me knowingly about things 'monastic'. I had never heard the adjective, and while I had heard of Matins I had no idea what or who they were. The next day I was in them. Fellow novices were Br Alban, Br Leo, who had left a modern religious order because it was not 'monastic' enough, Br Damian who kept referring everything back to some place called Quarr Abbey which he considered a 'real' monastery (I was confused: I only knew one real monastery, Belmont), and there was Br Gregory (McCarthy) who left at the end of the first year. (Did God send him just to jerk me in?) Outsiders would ask how I was settling in; I could only reply with some irony that I had not yet unpacked my suitcases. It was metaphorically true and remained a powerful metaphor thereafter as I grieved over a past so totally left behind and fantasies never realized. I resented wearing the habit: it was like a castration. If it was what God wanted then I would do it. I had no ideas beyond what my novice master said of where I was going or what for. Yet underneath all the doubt and confusion I felt a deep inner sense that it was 'good for me to be here', so it must be what God wanted even if I could make no sense of it. Who can, at age 18, make sense of a lifelong commitment? The only reality is the present moment; that is where it is good to be. God would show me the rest.

ENTER THE HOLY SPIRIT

In 1962 came the greatest event in the history of the world since the Council of Jerusalem of *c*. AD 48, the Second

169

Vatican Council. The Council ended in the autumn of 1965. That year I was sent to study Theology at the University of Fribourg, Switzerland. Now, 41 years after the end of the Council, no one who was not around then could understand the sheer power of the Spirit rushing through the churches. It was definitely good for us to be there. The speed with which the Spirit moved the hearts of those great bishops emerging from obscurity, the theologians, the liturgists and ecumenists, was like a cruise missile. It was indeed frightening to some but was new life to most. Now, instead of the Divine Office being prayed by rote, it became alive; the Mass became 'ours'. Out of the blue, my sister Georgina sent me a copy of the first edition of the *Grail* psalm translation which appeared during the Council and which left me with a new vision, that the psalms really could be prayed. Almost at once I found Psalm 62[63]:

O God, you are my God, for you I long, for you my soul is thirsting.
My body pines for you, like a dry weary land without water.
So I gaze on you in the sanctuary, to see your strength and your glory.
For your love is better than life, my lips will speak your praise.
So I will praise you all my life; in your name I will lift up my hands.

The psalmist is saying, 'Lord, it is good for me to be here.' I came to realize that contemplation was even for second-class junior monks like me, if they wanted it.

ENTER THE ANGEL

I loved Fribourg. Though a small, rather closed Catholic canton, the freedom it meant for me was overwhelming: the social life was surprisingly broad, the Scripture courses of Professors Spicq and Barthélemy were utterly inspiring and, above all, the spirit of the Second Vatican Council was wafting through. But all this time there was a dimension missing from my life. While at Fribourg I was invited to join the All Nations Student Association, an amorphous group of Anglophile students. Uncharacteristically, I arrived early for the first meeting. On walking into the room, I saw, sitting all alone in the middle of the middle row of not too many chairs, a gorgeous creature with a very pretty face, long loose reddish-brown hair, an elegant white crocheted dress and white high-heeled shoes, somewhat out of keeping for a student meeting. As the only other person in the room, I could hardly sit behind or in front or too far removed from her, so I sat at a respectable distance in the same row and conversation was joined – in French. Hers was so fluent that I took it for the real thing until, at about the time when others were entering and it seemed sensible and irresistible to close the gap between us, she revealed that she was in fact from Gloucestershire. I have always lived off coincidences. Her parents lived in Fribourg; her mother was French and her English father worked for some Catholic organization in the town. This goddess actually seemed to want to talk to me and I could not imagine what made me worthy. Although I soon discovered that her family background was as Catholic and protective as my monastic home, this was still not enough to make me worthy to discourse with a goddess, for I could see that she was not just ordinarily pretty, nor ordinarily intelligent.

Her name was Françoise and she had returned from

171

England to complete her final year of an English licentiate at the university under an eccentric ex-Cambridge professor named Smith whose only demand was that she translate Beowulf morning, noon and night. She found Smith an endearing old character, but at a mere 21 it seemed to her that there was more to life than Beowulf. I met her many times after this at her parents' house where her mother would indulge in ambivalent conversation pieces about how much she admired the dedication of the English Benedictine brothers, including me, but was there not just a possibility I might rethink the whole thing and take the hand of her '*petite Françoise*'? While I pondered this incessantly, Françoise, finally armed with her licentiate, slipped from the clutches of Beowulf and Smith to find herself a world, teaching in Germany.

UNWILLINGLY TO SCHOOL

Perhaps owing to all this elation and romance I returned to my monastery in 1969 sad and confused. I sensed that teaching in our monastery school was to be my lot and that was where it would all end. I had developed a taste for theology and Scripture which was going to be dissipated, I felt sure, by text-book teaching and rugby coaching. I liked my former school but something was coming between me and it, something spiritual and not clearly discernible. I asked the new abbot, Dom Robert Richardson, if I could work on the abbey's parish at Belmont. He told me that one of his school housemasters had just resigned and asked if I would take on Vaughan House. I had to understand it his way. I was only eight years older than the oldest boy and I felt instinctively inadequate. With this began a chain of jobs without choice, jobs taken on unwillingly, almost all of which I came to love and finally could scarcely bear to

172

leave. The boys were great and worked relentlessly to turn me into a rounded human being. After 14 years, I did not wish to admit that I was exhausted for fear of losing the job I had never wanted in the first place.

FROM THE DOLDRUMS TO FREE WILL

I met Françoise at various points in our friendship after Fribourg. Back at Belmont I grew to resent my monastic commitment. I reflected on how, before going to Fribourg, the abbot had intimated that he would not send me away until I had taken my Solemn Vows, 'in case you leave'. At the time, any cynicism was masked by my delight at being chosen to go. Now, back in the cloister, that abbot's reasoning began to fill me with resentment. Monks at Belmont seemed shell-shocked by what they took to be the effects of Vatican II. Two were in the process of leaving and my old novice master asked me in baleful tone, 'You're not leaving too, are you?' I returned to an atmosphere of mistrust: Br Simon has come back with all those new-fangled heresies. It was not that the community failed to accept Vatican II: no, the new abbot threw himself behind it, a new generation of junior monks completely revised the Divine Office and the church was disastrously reordered for the best of reasons. But so much was external: there was no place for even a very modest 'new theologian' like myself. In that atmosphere it was difficult not to daydream about an alternative world which revolved around Françoise.

Was it therefore surprising that when my two remaining colleagues, Damian and Leo, went forward to priestly ordination in 1967, I was not willing and had begun to see myself as a brother ... or even as a layman? Those doubts took on real meaning as my longing for Françoise grew in her absence. Distance was no obstacle, for we felt sure of our love, though neither of us from our Catholic straitjackets had ever admitted it. My hopes of working on the Belmont parish had hardly been realistic given my state of mind over the priesthood. Conversely, my appointment to the school led to such intense involvement that I scarcely had time to think about my doubts or about Françoise. The community was unhappy about my indecision, as were my parents. In the end, it was the boys who converted me, not by any outward evangelism, but their presence and their demands just led me gently towards the realization that in the kind of school we had and with the kind of boys they were, I could not do the job as then envisaged without being a priest; celebrating Mass with them was crucial. More and more God's touch was coming via other people.

In the scant moments of non-activity which remained for personal prayer, I had been absorbing St John's Gospel and was struck by the words:

> The Father loves me,
> because I lay down my life
> in order to take it up again.
> No one takes it from me;
> I lay it down of my own free will,
> and as it is in my power to lay it down,
> so it is in my power to take it up again;
> and this is the command I have been given by my
> Father.
>
> (Jn 10.17-18, JB)

I had never really noticed these words before. What attracted me was the extraordinary expression of Jesus' own freedom: that he did not have to lay down his life. I needed his reassurance: I did not have to lay down my life in this way. I did not have to be a priest. I did have freedom even within his creative plan. He knew how I was feeling and it was acceptable to say so. These words were written for every kind of spiritually 'mixed-up kid' like me who might be feeling that he was on a gravy train to a predetermined destination. Jesus really did have free will to lay down his life or not to lay it down, and also to take it up again. I reflected on Jesus' words in Gethsemane, 'Father, if it be possible let this chalice pass from me, yet let not my will but yours be done.' I began to repeat, by way of a mantra, those words of the 'Our Father', 'Thy will be done on earth as it is in Heaven'; without those words I could make no sense of my world.

Like Jesus, I needed to be empowered to lay down my life of my own free will. Seeing those words from St John as some kind of condition of service, I chose them as the text for my ordination cards complemented by a small print of Georges Rouault's 'Man of Sorrows'. To me it is not a man of sorrows but a man both terminally wounded and profoundly at peace with his decision to do his father's will. I too wanted that gift and began to see that those wounds must in some form or another be the price.

In the spring of 1972, I wrote to Françoise telling her of my decision to be ordained. She said she would like to come over and see me. It was 25 April. We went for a long walk over the Malvern Hills. Being the resilient Catholic she was, she accepted and entirely supported my decision. When we returned to Malvern station, as the train was on the verge of leaving, she suddenly planted a huge kiss on my lips and leapt into the train. That was affirmation; it's how women do it. I had received a touch of God from one of his angels. I don't remember anything of the drive back.

I was ordained on 4 May, the Feast of the Forty Martyrs, 1972. Not many years later, Françoise, still working in Germany, wrote to say that she was to marry Wilfried Lex,

175

a professor of mathematics and a most gentle and generous man. Without wishing to digress into a spiritual 'Mills & Boon', I would like to complete the story of Françoise because my search for God would not be complete without her. Several times I visited her and her new family in an obscure part of Saxony where, despite her loving household, she was very lonely, or they would come on holiday to England. Françoise and I would go for long walks and love was still there but could not be expressed. Something inside us made us completely faithful and respectful towards each other's commitment.

Françoise died of multiple brain tumours on 14 August 1999. She was 54. My only consolation was that I was able to see her in a clinic in Hildesheim a few days before, to anoint her and give her communion. I hope I was able to give some comfort to her family but since then my memory of her has gone strangely blank. I can't quite believe it happened.

During the 32 years I had known her we had each amassed a mutual correspondence as thick as a London telephone directory. We shared the same sense of humour, the same views on the Church (poor Church!) and on everything else. I often reflected that we should never have married because we were too alike but I would conclude that I am utterly convinced that God brought us into each other's lives and meant us to grow in love, in my case for the sake of my spiritual health, my ministry to others, especially to women, and to my monastic life. I don't know what I gave to her except that she went on seeking it. She taught me not to be afraid and that I could be loved, which years of monastic life had not revealed to me. Most of all she made me think of someone outside of myself. It was good for her to have been there.

PERU AND ALL THINGS NEW

In 1980, Belmont Abbey made a dependent monastic foundation in Peru. Monks were asked to volunteer. I had long been sympathetic to the idea but now, after 14 years as a housemaster and even whilst admitting that I was pretty exhausted and past my best, I was not so keen on Peru. However, I also felt that a community vote in favour was a calling to each of us so, like the son who said 'no', I went along to the abbot and volunteered, reasonably sure that he would leave me where I was. He did. Our first monks, Fathers Luke Waring, David Bird and Paul Stonham, established themselves first of all in a parish house in the small northern country town of Tambogrande where they distinguished themselves by their zeal for the local Church. But by 1982 Peru had become one of the unmentionable concepts of community consciousness. There was no long queue to go.

At the end of 1982, Abbot Jerome Hodkinson unexpectedly asked if I would like to go out for 'a holiday' – abbots have such a nice way of putting their intentions. Thinking no more of it, I said, 'Yes'. I was anxious to see this exciting new country: I had even spent some time the previous summer touring Spain with a grammar book just in case. I went, I saw and I pondered. I had some very memorable experiences but only days before leaving there began the worst rains in recorded history, attributed to the infamous El Niño current. With this threat of total inundation, I was glad to have a return ticket. I was still a child, *un niño*. The night I returned, the abbot scarcely mentioned Peru; he simply told me that the headmaster of the school had resigned and he asked me if I would take on the job. Not for the last time, here was a decision bordering on the absurd and I saw my inadequacy alongside the usual scene of there

177

being no one else available at the time. After a ritual 24 hours thinking-time, I returned to say, 'Yes'.

Although the job presented many encouraging challenges and although there were areas which, even on looking back, I feel I did correctly and well, nevertheless I felt I had been 'promoted to the level of my own incompetence'. While it came as a shock to me five years later when Abbot Alan Rees asked me to step down, it was something I was able to absorb with due common sense. Perhaps he and his advisers were wiser and perhaps it seemed an ideal moment to really send me to Peru – or anywhere! This decision changed my life because I felt a need for a medical check-up, a sensible step at 45, they say. I did not feel as actively fit as heretofore, yet I continued to play 'pretend' with sport coaching and other physical activities which I felt would help the school. I was ill-prepared for the specialist's diagnosis that I had a serious problem of angina and ought not to go to Peru. That warning was simultaneously a relief and another shock. I was just getting used to the new vision, and now what? The abbot kindly gave me a sabbatical year, asking me only if I would spend three months in Peru to give one of the others a holiday. This autobiography might seem to have been straying from the touch of God, but in fact it is precisely in these moments of the wholly unexpected that I have come to realize more and more that God was behind them all. I had never forgotten the message of Fr Hilary when I was at school that each of us has a unique vocation from God and if you don't fulfil yours, no one else ever will. God seemed to be asking something profound, and the more confused the picture, the more really it seemed to correspond to my discernment of his nature.

I spent the first three months of my sabbatical in the city of Granada, Spain, learning Spanish and drooling over the beauty of the Alhambra, then five months in London, enjoying the hospitality of Ealing Abbey and doing adult art classes at a variety of London schools, something I had always longed to do and at which I seemed to fare well. Finally, in the summer of 1989, I went to Peru where I assumed a sort of 'sugar-daddy' superiorship of two Peruvian novices, Luis and Sigfredo, who looked after me as if I were their poodle. More than anywhere else before, it was here that I came to realize the wonderful privilege of being a priest: that one is not just a tourist, one has an immediate passport to other people's hearts and homes, whatever their culture. One is a foreigner but the Church makes one universal, one of them. Some eight years later I was privileged to visit the Benedictine monastery in Tororo, Uganda, and experienced exactly the same when celebrating the sacraments in remote banana plantation churches.

RETREATANTS, PARISHIONERS AND A GREEK REVIVAL

Returning from Peru, I was appointed guest master of the monastery. Here I met a completely different clientele, some very gifted, some very needy, many very holy, many with demands I could scarcely meet, all with a deeper message for my own spiritual growth. But in 1994, another change at the top meant another change for me, Parish Priest of the Belmont Abbey parish, that which I had presumptuously coveted back in 1969.

Parish life meant a whole new challenge and a whole new set of relationships. Belmont Abbey parish is almost entirely rural. Parish visiting was an unmatchable visual delight and the friendship I met, even from the many lapsed Catholics, was deeply moving. With the mere 300 or so families spread over about 400 square miles of

179

gorgeous verdant Herefordshire, even in three years I could hardly cover a fractional part of those on the register, but every visit was a joy. Then, just as I was hoping to stay in this post forever, a problem had developed, leaving a vacancy at the neighbouring parish of St Francis Xavier in Hereford city. I had by this time been appointed Dean of the Herefordshire parishes and knew instinctively that I was going to have to fill this vacancy at what was the principal parish of the deanery. Another big penny dropped. It was the abbot's decision but this was something I had been dreading: I had no desire to move and certainly no desire to take on the current problems of that parish. It was on the last evening of a visit to Uganda and Kenya in 1997 that I received an abbatial telephone call (always to be suspected) in Nairobi to ask me if I would move. In that type of call the word 'ask' is a euphemism for 'instruct'. I returned to pack up and move. The fine Greek-revival church was in desperate need of repair and the archbishop asked me to undertake the work about which there was no small element of dissent. It was a daunting prospect but also a challenge, especially as I could draw upon a good deal of personal knowledge of architectural history. However, none of that material challenge could match the parochial challenge of a new, largely unknown city-centre congregation. If the prospect seemed daunting, the people were not, and I soon grew to love that parish and all about it, including the work on the church. I was also lucky to have an experienced and congenial assistant priest, Fr Stephen Holdsworth. God turned my fear to joy.

However, my capricious God was not going to allow me to sink into satisfaction. After three years, my abbot, Dom Mark Jabalé, was suddenly translated as bishop to the diocese of Menevia, South Wales, and the abbot chosen to replace him was Dom Paul Stonham, superior of our monastery in Peru. Another large penny dropped. I just took one look around and knew what was to be my next job. I had Spanish, I had been there before, my number was about to be called, my heart sank. As I talked with the new abbot over lunch that same day God gave me an extraordinary power to take the initiative and to ask him if he wanted me to go, knowing full well the answer. Now 12 years further down the angina trail and a year short of a bypass operation this God was urging me to go to the north Peruvian desert to lead a group of total unknowns in the incipient stages of their monastic life. The dear people of St Francis Xavier's were very understanding. Both they and I seemed to share my sense of leaving the planet Earth. The great spiritual writer, Jean-Pierre de Caussade (1675–1751), in his *Abandonment to Divine Providence*, summed up my sentiments three centuries ago:

> No matter what it is we attach ourselves to, God will step in and upset our plans so that, instead of peace, we shall find ourselves in the midst of confusion, trouble and folly. As soon as we say, 'I must go this way, I must consult this person, I must act like this,' God at once says the opposite and withdraws his power from those means which we ourselves have chosen. So we discover the emptiness of all created things, and are forced to turn to God and be content with him.
>
> (Chapter 4, Section 2)[1]

PERU AGAIN, THIS TIME THE BYPASS ROUTE

My new introduction to Peru was tragi-comic. I spent a preliminary six months with the Missionaries of the Society of St James the Apostle in Lima with a group of priests

181

mainly from the USA, Ireland and England, and a more amusing, wise and valiant group I will never again expect to meet. With them I enjoyed the best education to the Peruvian Church and politics I could hope for. I felt very humble in their presence. Meanwhile, I had managed to bring a small number of personal articles for general living and hobbies, lest I go mad. Of these I was generously relieved by armed robbers as they (the goods!) were being transported in the abbot's car to our monastery in Piura Province, 1000 km to the north. 'No purse, no haversack for you, my son!' said God. 'But God, they got my Jerusalem Bible, my theology books, my teaching notes for the novices and my oil paints.' 'I'm sure they'll know exactly what to do with those', I could hear Him saying. Finally, I went up myself to be greeted by a cheerful bunch of young monks at Piura airport. By 9 p.m. we arrived at my new monastery. I was mentally exhausted: life looked charcoal-grey. There was nothing for it but to pray and pray ... and pray. It wasn't piety, it was desperation.

> O how could we sing
> the song of the Lord
> on alien soil?

> (Ps. 136[137].4)

The Israelites tried it in Babylon: I tried it in Piura: it still worked. About 36 hours later a glimmer of light seemed to be piercing the monastic sky. It was good for me to be there.

ANOTHER PLANET

Space does not allow me to give further details about my life in Peru. I had expected to be there about ten years or until the fourth rider of the Apocalypse called me out. In fact I had been there just under five years when I received another abbatial phone call. Perhaps he was coming out unexpectedly to correct all the abuses. With my Nairobi experience I should have guessed, but this call was different. A curious influence over the Belmont telephone system made it such that I could hear him but he could not hear me. Was there a switch he did not know about ... or that he did know about? The Abbot President was going to phone me in a few days, he told me, to ask me whether I would go to ... 'Where!? He's mad. I've just settled in here', I was saying to a deaf receiver. I knew that only my capricious God could land me in this mire and then give me the courage to say, 'Yes'.

'Where?' turned out to be Washington DC, USA, to a monastery of quiet Americans belonging to the English Benedictine Congregation which seemed to be in need of a new superior and the injection of what one of them called 'a new chemical mix'. At age 75 and after 16 years on the throne, their recently retired abbot had more than merited a life of tranquillity. I was to be their Prior Administrator for the next four years. Having left planet Earth for Mars, I was now leaving for Venus: the north Peruvian desert and Washington DC have little in common. All I will say at this point is that, so far, the inmates are 'treating me nice' as I take each day at a time. This is a formed community, of men mostly older than myself, of different nationality and from a slightly different monastic tradition than what I am used to. I don't think I am here to reform them, though they are perhaps not yet ready for the Carthusian motto of *Nunquam reformata quia nunquam deformata* ('never reformed because never deformed'). I think I must be here simply to love them and lead them. Once again, it is good for me to be here.

DRAWING IN THE THREADS

Now I must bring a few threads together by way of conclusion. In this essay, I am very aware of having glossed over huge amounts of colour, supporting personalities and scenes from my text. Space just does not permit more. My kaleidoscope of present moments, of spontaneous and affectionate people, is to me so brilliant that, if God had also given me a memory, I could write a book. (On my first visit to Peru in 1982 I did write quite a colourful daily diary. The armed robbers of 2001 had that.) Let me here take up again two further texts from de Caussade:

> Every moment we live through is like an ambassador who declares the will of God, and our hearts always utter their acceptance. Our souls steadily advance, never halting, but sweeping along with every wind. Every current technique thrusts us upwards in our voyage to the infinite. Everything works to this end and, without exception, helps us towards holiness.
>
> (Chapter 2, Section 10)

All, that is, if we truly abandon ourselves to Divine Providence. It's a wonderful vision; would that that were true of me. Yet I can say that through no merit of my own and despite prolonged phases of resistance, I do believe that I have been touched by God's appeal, his challenges, by the obviousness and the craziness of his calls beyond any ounce of personal worth.

De Caussade again:

> It is what happens moment by moment which enlightens us and gives us that practical knowledge which Jesus himself chose to acquire before beginning

184

his public life. This knowledge that comes to us only through experience is absolutely necessary if we want to touch the hearts of those God sends us.

(Chapter 2, Section 8)

With all this unwarranted gift, just what have I done for others? Certainly, others have touched me, as I have shown, but have I really touched them and, if not, what was the point of it all? During my life, from signing up for God, I have come into contact with so many people outside my immediate family and fellow monks: there have been, and still are, school friends, university friends, parishioners, Peruvians, retreatants, hitch-hiking friends, friends from every walk of life. It is not only God who amazes me but them. They still seem to want to see me and respond to my letters and emails. They don't need to send me Christmas cards but they do and sometimes get one in return. They don't even seem to mind my turning up for a visit. Some of these I have known for over 50 years and they still seem as content with the friendship as I am. This is not a boast; I just marvel because I am not the sort of person I would be friends with or even write a card to.

But does this mean that I have touched them as they have me? After all, we share the same God. But have I just used their company and kept the source of salvation to myself? Have I listened to their inner need to know God and, if so, have I been up to guiding them when their lives often seem so immersed in the materialism which I have been able to ... yes, escape? Has *He* been a living element in our conversation or someone kept under wrappers for fear of embarrassment? Have I, in de Caussade's words, helped any of them to holiness, however unconsciously – which it usually is? My daily prayer covers them like a radar scanner but how much can one really be there for them, for everyone?

So, back to me. Why me? Why all those semi-disreputables in the Old Testament: Jacob, David, Jonah? Just to think back over the human opportunities, the enjoyment and the freedom makes me realize how uniquely blessed I have been by God. I do not think I would ever have been so happy in another walk of life, despite my many attempts to walk away from this one. For all this I have done nothing; I have merely been the son who said 'No', and never really unpacked his suitcases. I sometimes wonder whether, had I said 'Yes', and also been willing to go, God would have called me in the first place. Oh, life is funny!

The telephone is ringing. It must be God. I'd better go!

NOTES

1.   The extracts from Jean-Pierre de Caussade's *Abandonment to Divine Providence* are taken from the translation by John Beevers (1975). New York: Doubleday.

9

'All Manner of Things Shall be Well'

Monica Mead

I WILL MAKE ALL THINGS NEW

On the Feast of the Transfiguration in 2002 an elderly woman of 74 made her Solemn Profession in the Community of Our Lady Help of Christians, Chester. A little too old to begin a new life, you might think. Maybe, or was she finally fulfilling her vocation? What had led me to stand in the doorway of our chapel, ready and anxious to respond to the call of Christ? To the words, 'Come my daughter', I answered, moving into that sacred space: 'Now with all my heart I follow you.'

If I had been asked that day how it had all come about, it would have been impossible to say. I really did not know, only that it was right, that it had to be done. I was aware that my whole self would move forward into a new and irrevocable relationship with God and this monastic community. All the past, the greater part of my life, with its consequences, would remain with me, for monastic profession is traditionally deemed a deepening of baptism. I thought of the words of Julian of Norwich:

Sin is behovely [of use], but all shall be well and all
shall be well and all manner of things shall be well.
(Revelations of Divine Love,
Thirteenth Revelation, ch. 27)

HOW IT ALL BEGAN

It is not possible for me to write this from the same
perspective as the contributors to *A Touch of God*. Most of
them had been called to the monastic life in their youth. I
had lived in the world for almost 70 years. Yet the
preparation for my life in the monastery had begun long
ago. I did not find it difficult adapting to monastic life: it all
seemed quite natural to me. I had learned a similar form of
obedience, and the need for silence, when working in an old-
fashioned type of stables. Unexpected noise would frighten
the horses, as idle chatter can scatter recollection. No
raucous laughter was permitted, and the horses needed a
regular routine and discipline as much as we do for our
monastic life. Later, I worked aboard ships where the
captain's word was law. One did not question commands:
one obeyed.

My parents were nominally Church of England, but
never attended church. Later in life my mother would
sometimes 'go to church', but not on a regular basis. Like
most middle-class children in the 1930s we were told Bible
stories, and said our prayers before going to bed. Mother
was a very quiet person who devoted herself to her children.
Father did not feature much in my early childhood,
although he must have shown some interest in his two
daughters. I can recollect crying after him when he left
home one morning to go to work. I was really rather afraid
of him, he shouted so much when he was angry. Perhaps my
later image of an angry God was unconsciously influenced

by him. Sometimes, when my father was at home on a Sunday, we would all go out for a drive in the car. He must have been a difficult man to live with, and I don't think it was a happy marriage. My parents divorced later on.

Mother was a moral person, who disliked any form of lies. She always said to us that whatever we did, we would be forgiven if we told the truth. This was an excellent preparation for confession, although I did not know this until much later in life. I think my mother showed great wisdom in dealing with her children. I was very independent, strong-willed and stubborn but she usually managed to persuade me to her way of thinking. She was so gentle in doing this that I was not aware of it. She thus avoided head-on collisions with me, which would simply have made me more obstinate. Just before my sixth birthday, I was sent to a private preparatory school. It was a small school, with only two classrooms. The children were divided into groups according to age and ability. I was there for five years and loved it as I was interested and eager to learn. Those were the days of patriotism, when we celebrated Empire Day and our national saints. Again, the appreciation of good people who had influenced our national life prepared me for the lives of saints and their influence upon the Church. We were given a very sound basic education, which was just as well: those five years were the only consecutive schooling that my sister and I had. After that, for one reason or another, only partially owing to the Second World War, our schooling was frequently interrupted.

From earliest childhood I was aware that God existed. I can't remember a time when he was not there. I perceived him as all-powerful, and believed that he could get angry and punish those who sinned. I attended Sunday School for a time, and sometimes went to church for Evening Prayer with an aunt whom we visited on Sundays. I always thought

189

of this as a great treat and loved the solemnity of it all. I also enjoyed singing hymns with a lady lodger at my grandmother's place who listened to a religious radio programme. We followed the words from one of her hymn books. I have always found the poetry of hymns full of meaning: are hymns our version of the Psalms? I acquired most of my religious knowledge at that little school; it stayed with me always, even when I turned away from God. I felt that he let me go my own way, but kept drawing me back to him with the leading reins of love (cf. Hos. 11.4).

TRAGEDIES AND THE WAR

As I lived on the coast and in a major port (Liverpool), the sea was always important to me. In 1939 there was a terrible tragedy in our area. The new submarine, *Thetis*, pride of the Royal Navy at the time, went on diving trials in Liverpool Bay. There was a series of accidents or errors and the submarine sank, killing 99 people. What I found so dreadful was that the tail of the submarine was raised above water-level yet the trapped men inside could not be freed. It brought home to me in a frightening way the feebleness of man: only God could have helped. Why didn't he?

We went on holiday to France that year, and during a visit to the Louvre, one painting was imprinted on my mind. It showed a shipwreck in the middle distance and in the foreground a large raft, laden with dead or dying people, some floating or swimming round it; just a mass of people, a heap of humanity. I thought of the *Thetis* and that real pile of men entombed in the submarine. Where was God? Twelve years later, I returned to the Louvre and found the painting again. Somehow it failed to touch me as it had previously. Perhaps the War, with its terrifying pictures, had made me less sensitive. The painting was *The Raft of the*

190

Medusa by Gericault, inspired by an actual shipwreck. That shipwreck created a scandal in France, which the *Thetis* did not in England. The *Thetis* was eventually salvaged, renamed *HMS Thunderbolt*, and in 1943, was depth-charged by an Italian ship off Sicily with the loss of all hands.

The so-called 'phoney war' (1939–40), was an unsettled time. My father was at a loose end, his business at a standstill. He had volunteered for the army but was not accepted then on health grounds. My grandparents and parents decided to take a holiday in the south of France. Our return to England was delayed as my grandfather was taken ill. Mother was torn between concern for her father and the safety of her children. Once my grandfather was out of danger we drove hurriedly across France to St Malo, very conscious of the proximity of the war zone. We had to wait there for a ship as all seaworthy craft were involved in the evacuation of Dunkirk. There were long queues winding up and down the quay outside the shipping office every morning. We would wait patiently with all the other people until we were informed that there would be no ship that day. We waited for some six days. When a ship came – rudely called 'a glorified cattle-boat' – the authorities allowed as many as could be safely transported on board. It was an overnight run to Southampton. I don't think many people slept that night. It was all a bit frightening but exciting for us children. Mother was a tower of strength. We knew that the German army was moving towards Paris, but her quiet courage allayed our own fears. Did I see in my mother an image of Our Lady, quiet and strong in times of stress?

Father was accepted for the army when we returned to England. We moved to a different part of Liverpool, where we started at another convent school just across the road from us. There were a lot of air raids that winter. Mother again gave us confidence, assuring us that all would be well. We stayed in Liverpool until after the May Blitz, when Father, on leave that weekend, insisted on our moving to Southport away from the bombs. I was very sorry to leave Bellerive Convent as I had settled in well. Both Reverend Mother and I tried to persuade my parents to let me travel each day from Southport but they would not permit this. They considered it would be too dangerous as I would have been returning home at dusk, just the time of air raids.

The War brought many changes to all our lives. During the next three years (1940–43), until I was 14, my sister and I attended three different Catholic convent schools. My parents did not expect or want us to gain knowledge of Catholicism but it was impossible to spend our days in that environment without becoming aware of at least some of the teachings of the Church. This seemed to give more meaning to what I had already learned, and remained with me throughout life. At school I was always somewhat envious of the Catholic girls: I was told that their religion was the only true one.

REBELLION AND FAMILY PROBLEMS

All this change was bad for me and I rebelled by not applying myself to work. I began to have bad migraines. I had always wanted to go to university to earn a Bachelor of Science degree, and then to teach. However, the consultant we saw advised my parents that my health was not adequate for this. I was very disappointed but did not repine. When 'one door closed, God opened another'. With hindsight, I came to recognize the generosity and mercy of God's dealings with me. My sister and I were having riding lessons. Seeing our keen interest, our parents bought us ponies. Looking after them and helping out in the stables was both great fun and healthy for me. I was out in the fresh air more, as the doctor had suggested. Horses and ponies filled our lives until there was no room for anything else.

Money was tight after Father went into the army. My parents decided that mother should take on a small market town hotel in Uttoxeter. So our lives were disrupted again. As long as we girls were with the horses we were happy. After the War we went to an equestrian establishment in Sussex to work for our Institute of the Horse certificates, which involved training in stable management, veterinary first aid and equestrian skills.

My parents' relationship continued to deteriorate. Rows began unnecessarily: a different answer could have prevented them arising. I saw that quarrels are always two-sided, and never resolve any situation. As a result, I have always tried to avoid quarrelling. But silence can also be harmful.

My parents divorced when I was 18. I, being of an independent nature and knowing that it was no use wasting time grumbling, took practical action: I advertised in the *Horse and Hound* and found a job. It was what I wanted to do anyway, and removed me from an intolerable situation. Thus I would not have to choose between my parents. Of course my father objected strongly but I just went ahead and worked for a dealer in horses in the West Country.

MARRIAGE AND SEPARATION

It was in Somerset that I met my future husband and was introduced to the farming community in that area. It was a good time as I'd always hankered after a country life, even as a little girl. All this seemed like a dream coming true. Going to church on Sunday evenings was all part of country life. I joined with my fiancé's family in attending evening service on Sundays. I always tended to take things seriously and so gave a great deal of thought to what I was doing. I decided that I would like to be confirmed, and attended classes. I didn't at that time recognize the distinctive characteristics of different types of Christianity. I had been baptized into the Church of England as an infant and did not think of changing my religion. It was as though an Englishman were to decide to become Welsh or Scottish: it wasn't possible. So I was confirmed into the Church of England just before my twenty-first birthday.

My attitude to marriage was strongly influenced by Catholicism and the attitude at that time to divorce. I saw marriage as a serious commitment, involving a total giving of myself to my husband and any family we might have. I was a happy idealist, convinced I could make our marriage work. I had not yet learnt that without God I could do nothing, for, as Origen wrote, 'There would be no need for the Holy Spirit if we could become holy in our own strength, but God has sent him to our aid because we cannot.' That was a lesson which would take me many more years to learn. I looked forward to a large family, taking it for granted that my husband, a farmer, felt the same. We had been married for 13 months when our first son was born. He was warmly welcomed. I became pregnant again five months later, but our second son did not receive the same warm welcome and sought his father's love in vain for the rest of his life. The question of contraception arose. This was totally unacceptable to me. I believed contraception to be contrary to God's law and yet I had promised obedience to my husband. I was in a cleft stick. I was only allowed to conceive again three years later, and bore our third son. After another period of four years, our little girl was born. I very much resented my own obedience in this matter, and my husband and I drifted further and further apart. I had obeyed to try and save our marriage but the psychological toll eventually became too much. Our second son developed epilepsy at the age of 11. He had always been a difficult child, given to destructive tempers. Epilepsy seemed to make this worse. His violence could be frightening and his medication did not seem to help. My son and I visited many specialists and psychiatrists, and he spent six weeks in the National Hospital for Nervous Diseases: all to no avail. I was then told that he was schizophrenic.

I felt very much alone with my son. Nobody took the threat of potential violence seriously. He was an intelligent child, and had done well at his preparatory school. A doctor from the Hospital for Nervous Diseases advised me to send my son as arranged to the boarding school for which we had entered him some years previously. Ten days later the Headmaster asked me to take him away as younger children were not safe with him. Matters went from bad to worse. I suffered from great anxiety when my second son went out alone and yet I could not accompany him everywhere; he was a growing teenager wanting the freedom of his contemporaries. I never knew if or when he would become violent. I knew that my other children were being neglected during the holidays, especially my small daughter. My husband seemed to disassociate himself from the situation. Something in me finally snapped. One morning I woke up a different person, quietly determined to leave my husband, realizing he would probably divorce me after the prescribed legal time, even though divorce was morally abhorrent to me, and still is. In later years when I read of St Paul's 'inward struggle' in his Letter to the Romans, I saw with the utmost clarity that this described my own state of mind at that time:

We know that the Law is spiritual; but I am carnal,
sold under sin. I do not understand my own actions.
For I do not do what I want, but I do the very thing I
hate ... I agree that the Law is good. So, then, it is no
longer I that do it, but sin which dwells within me.

(Rom. 7.14-17)

The two other boys were away at school; they could join me
for their holidays. Our daughter would come with me, and
also our epileptic son – if he wanted to. My father owned a
yacht based in the Mediterranean and I knew there was no
cook-steward on board. I could cook and clean. In a matter
of a few days it was all worked out in my head; there were
no discussions or arguments. I just told my husband and my
parents what my plans were and left with the two children.

How had I become like this? I don't know, it was totally
out of character. I had tried so hard to be obedient, quietly
coping with acute problems, but it wasn't enough. I had no
strength left. I did believe in God, but I didn't expect him to
help me.

The sharpest pangs we feel are not those of the body,
nor those of the estate, but those of the mind ... The
spirit of a man will sustain his infirmity, but a
wounded spirit, who can bear? ... You may have no
outward cause whatever for sorrow, and yet if the
mind be dejected, the brightest sunshine will not
relieve your gloom.

(C. H. Spurgeon, *Sermons* Vol. 11.)

Several more years had to pass by before I could accept
assistance from God.

LIMBO AND GLIMPSES OF HEAVEN

I lived on board the yacht for two years and thoroughly enjoyed it. Although there were other crew members, as well as guests and my own family on board, I felt a great sense of freedom and glorious isolation at sea. It was another world. Standing in the bows, leaning against the stem as the ship cleaves the waters is an incredible experience. The forward motion through the air draws all sound away: the only sound comes from the sea itself, and one feels suspended, solitary, flying like a bird over the water. The vastness and power of the Creator is overwhelming, as it can be on a mountain top. Deep silence is more than just the absence of sound. I was reminded of this when we watched one of the television programmes of *The Monastery* in 2005. A monk spoke to the 'novices' as they sat quietly in the church: 'Listen, can't you hear it?' A pause, then, 'The Silence.' He's right: it *is* possible to hear silence.

This was a strange time in my life: I was happy but life had a dream-like quality of unreality. I saw myself, watched myself, as though I were two separate people. One was a woman who had left her husband and children and was divorced. The other found such behaviour unacceptable and yet could do nothing about it. So she watched herself in dismay and disbelief but could not bring herself to turn back, even for the sake of the children. To the best of my ability I tried to limit the damage to the children. However, four years had to pass before I began to feel a whole person again. I had abandoned all my responsibilities and it was only slowly that I could start to shoulder them once more.

197

MALTA

My father wanted to start a new company in Malta, where the yacht was based. He was beginning his fly-cruise programme and wanted to use Malta as the main supply port. He needed an office there to deal with the purchasing and deliveries to the ship, all of which had to be done by tender as the vessel was too large to come alongside. The currency was Sterling, which was also convenient for monies both on and off the ship. He sold the yacht but asked me to stay in Malta as his representative both on board and on the island. I did this gladly. The two younger children loved coming out to Malta during their school holidays. The older boys were less at ease with me and did not visit so regularly.

I was very much at home in Malta. The Maltese were devout Catholics. No one seemed to do anything without first making the sign of the Cross. On feast days there were religious processions with statues. God was always present to them in a way I had never seen before. One could not ignore this sense of God's presence in their lives. As I began to settle down after the upheaval in my life there came a great desire to make contact with God again. I did not think it possible, after all I had done, but I wanted God. I thought that my behaviour could not be forgiven because I could not make adequate reparation. I still had no idea what Christianity was all about. As I was unacceptable to myself, so I expected the same disapproval from God. However, he sought me out, one of the many lost sheep his Son came to bring back to the flock.

As the Mediterranean shipping world was not used to dealing with a woman at that time, it was necessary to have a figurehead. My father asked the merchant navy skipper who had worked for him previously on the yacht to fill this figurehead role in Malta. I enjoyed being separate from the rest of the world. One was very aware that all that one ate or used was brought by sea: the island is not self-sufficient in any way. Did not John Donne write that 'no man is an island' as we are not self-sufficient but always need to rely on God and other human beings? I remember one occasion when it was impossible to purchase sugar. The ship had been delayed. This reminded me of the hardships the heroic Maltese people endured during the last War.

During these years in Malta I met my second husband. We married in a registry office in England at my husband's request. I thought that my first marriage, even though it was not a Catholic marriage, could not be dissolved. So I thought I was still married before God and committing adultery. I only discovered later that I had been mistaken in this. At the time, our living together was my commitment to a human other, and I still felt cut off from God.

DISINTEGRATION

My husband and I had to earn our own living, and we turned to catering work. My epileptic son was at a loose end as another of the attempts to give him some training and independence had failed. He came to live with us, and to help when he was well. My husband was good with him but had underlying doubts about his condition, particularly when we discovered that my son possessed a flick-knife from which he refused to be parted. I was the only person my son would listen to, and then not always. One day he attacked me. My husband heard me call out, and there was a dreadful fight. Eventually peace was restored, but I knew that this attack on me had changed the situation. Whatever control I had had was gone. A few days later, as I was working in the kitchen, my son was picking up large kitchen knives and then replacing them. There was a challenge in his attitude, as he said 'Things are different now, aren't they Mum?'

A week later matters did get out of control. My son attacked my husband with a knife. I called the police as a last resort. They took my son away and he was put on remand pending medical investigation. This dreadful situation was resolved, but in a way I could not have anticipated. At nine o'clock the following morning a policeman knocked on the door to inform me my son had died about an hour previously. His heart, which unbeknown to us, was weak from constant fits, had stopped while he was dressing himself. He was 20 years of age. I knew in one way it was merciful, and I prayed that it had been quick for his sake. He would have been so frightened had he realized what was happening to him. I felt that God was cruel to take him in these circumstances: why did he have to die alone and apparently abandoned by me? Was I thus meant to learn the anguish of countless mothers whose sons had died alone in even more terrible circumstances? I do not know.

In *Candles in the Dark* Amy Carmichael wrote:

> The one person who stands out in my memory as one incapable of ever helping others was the one who never suffered – never even had a headache ... I have often thought of her and been thankful for pain.
>
> (p. 9)

We carried on with the catering. If anything I was working harder than ever; it was the only way I could cope. A few years later my father asked us to act as his representatives on board a Bulgarian ship he was chartering. This meant trying to learn at least a smattering of the language, as the crew was Bulgarian. It was difficult in a short space of time to learn a new language with a new alphabet, but we spent three months in London doing our best. It was even harder than the Latin I tried to learn when I entered the monastery!

When we returned to England I again had a strong longing to be in communion with God. My daughter was to be confirmed, and the Anglican bishop allowed me to receive communion with her. But I did not think that I could be a full member of the Church again.

MAJORCA

By now we were concerned about my husband's health. He was in the first stages of progressive Parkinson's disease, so we decided to retire to Majorca, where my parents had now settled, having been reconciled and remarried. We found a little house in a country area with some land and a share in an almond orchard. My husband loved growing things. The holding was small but enough for us, with fig, orange, lemon and pomegranate trees. Then my father died, and as our little finca was becoming too much for my husband to cope with, we decided to move nearer to my mother's home, overlooking the sea.

An Anglican priest was once staying with my mother and asked me to drive him to the Anglican chapel for the Sunday morning service. I asked if I could accompany him. I there met the chaplain and his wife who were very encouraging and helpful. Through them I came to a greater understanding of God's great love and tenderness in his dealings with the human race. Things that had only been concepts before began to have a real meaning.

One Sunday the chaplain included in his sermon a paragraph from a book by Catherine Marshall. I was very impressed and managed to find a copy. After I had read some of Catherine Marshall's books, it seemed to me that the only reparation I could offer the people I had hurt through my actions was to write letters of apology. I did this. I began to think differently about God the Father: he was no longer wrathful but a God of compassion and mercy – a God who wanted to forgive. But I still thought I had to make reparation. The Good News that Christ came to save sinners had still not touched me. I was an unwitting disciple of Pelagius, thinking my own efforts were required. Still, I was drawn to read other Christian writers. Mother Teresa of Calcutta and Pope John Paul II became icons for me. I began to think 'if only . . .'

Something wonderful happened at this time. I had been an addicted smoker for more than 20 years, smoking some 50 cigarettes a day. My husband did not smoke. I had tried to give it up, always without success. One day, when I wanted to find a little extra money for a charity, a very clear voice seemed to come from the direction of the window, saying 'Give up smoking'. This was so real that I answered quite vehemently, 'You know that I can't do that. If you want me to stop smoking you will have to deal with it yourself.' That was all, but the unbelievable happened. I have never since had the slightest desire to smoke another cigarette. Perhaps because I had put myself into his hands, God had accepted the challenge and removed the craving for tobacco. It was completely gone. Without knowing, I had discovered the truth of the words Our Lord spoke to Saint Paul: 'My grace is sufficient for you for my power is made perfect in weakness' (2 Cor. 12.9).

I was always happier in a Catholic environment. As a child I sought out Catholic churches to visit both at home and abroad: I was immediately attracted to Catholic characters in books. As an adult I purchased Catholic religious objects: a crucifix rather than a cross, and I had a rosary to pray with. In Majorca the Anglican community functioned by courtesy of the Spanish State and Church, so there seemed to be a Catholic connection. What a disappointment when I returned to England and could not find the Catholic ethos in the Anglican Church I was attending. Yet my life in England was not without joy: it was good to see more of my children and their families. But my husband's health continued to fail. We had been together 23 years when he died.

> God did not make the first man because he needed company, but because he wanted someone to whom he could show his generosity and love. God did not tell us to follow him because he needed our help but because he knew that serving him would make us whole.
>
> (Irenaeus, *Against the Heresies*, IV.14.1)

TAKING THE PLUNGE

One day, glancing through the morning papers a couple of years later, I noticed a small advertisement for the Catholic Truth Society. It flashed through my mind that I must write for more information. (I had realized by this time that people did convert from one religion to another.) I wrote, and eagerly awaited the reply. Maybe, just maybe, I might be able to become a Catholic. I really can't begin to describe what this meant to me. When my little packet arrived I read the material avidly, and then contacted our Catholic parish priest in Somerset, where I was then living. I made the appointment, and one afternoon in January 1995 found myself standing at the door of the priest's house. I felt nervous as I had no idea of what to expect. We talked, and I told him something of my life and the areas that I felt might present problems. My instruction in the Catholic faith had begun, and I was received into the Catholic Church in May 1995.

At about this time I had a very real dream, the sort of dream which is never forgotten. It was completely real to me, especially in its spiritual significance. I used to think that if only my second son had been different, maybe I would not have left husband and children all those years ago. I was not exactly blaming the boy for events but I did think his illness was contributory. In some way, I was holding him responsible for my action.

In my dream I was swimming in a river between high buildings. A strong current was carrying me. The basements of these buildings were in the river. I was suddenly swept to where I could see archways below the waterline. I saw the face of my son pressed against a glass barrier, his mouth was pressed against the glass, with the same longing look that children have when they see what they desire. I felt impelled to set him free by opening the window. He shot forth with a great whoosh and was carried swiftly down the river, out of sight. It reminded me of another birth.

I thought about it for several days. I wondered whether I had kept my son prisoner through my unwitting resentment, and had now finally released him. Had we been bound together through my resentment? I was now able to recognize what I had done and had become free. Free myself, I could now set him free, and love him again as I had when he was a little child. The prophet Hosea had portrayed God as an anguished parent:

When Israel was a child I loved him ...
They did not know that I was the one caring for them,
... leading them with human ties,
with leading-strings of love ...
that ... I was like someone lifting an infant to his cheek,
and that I bent down to feed him.

(drawn from Hos. 11.1-4, NJB)

My friend, an oblate of Downside Abbey, suggested I accompany her to meetings there. I became very interested and eventually was accepted as an oblate myself. One of the monks became my spiritual director. It was about that time that I saw the *Everyman* programme 'Suburban Sisters' on BBC 2, little realizing that, one day, I would be a member of that same Benedictine community featured in the programme. I read the *Rule of St Benedict* and some commentaries, and books about the contemplative life. I was aware that something in me was not satisfied, that I needed something more. This longing for something deeper and more meaningful in life would not leave me. I began to wonder if God was trying to tell me something through this longing. Did I have a vocation to the monastic life? That seemed very improbable. I told myself 'Don't be silly, at your age, with your past life. Your first husband is still alive. It's quite ridiculous.' But the idea just would not leave me alone. I saw that I could not resolve this by myself: I needed advice and help. This was a breakthrough: when had I ever sought or accepted help before?

I asked my spiritual director for advice. After some months he suggested I should write and make enquiries about the possibility of entering monastic life. When I asked 'Where?' he said 'Begin with the Abbess of Curzon Park, Chester.' I wrote, and met the abbess and the community. I spent some time with them as an aspirant, and because the community had had a very good experience with their choir oblate, Sister Maria Conze, who entered aged 66, I was accepted as a postulant choir oblate.

I entered on 13 January 1997. I was so HAPPY – for several weeks it seemed my feet never touched the ground – it was unbelievable – I was here living in God's house! The wonder of it is still with me. As it happened, I was permitted to make Solemn Profession in the monastic life in 2002. I had obtained a Canonical Dispensation (as my first husband was still alive), first from the Bishop of the Diocese of Shrewsbury, and then from Rome.

MONASTIC LIFE

Anyone who reads this will appreciate that I am not a natural writer. I cannot verbalize my experiences, and often it is only through the writings of other people, and most especially the Scriptures, that I can articulate what I most deeply feel. I remain largely self-contained, although I enjoy conversation. As a child, I was called 'the absent-minded professor'. This characteristic of absent-mindedness, or absorption in something other than the matter in hand, is noted by others but I am unconscious of this, and puzzled by it. God had caught hold of me as a child, and all through my life, he had nudged me back to the right road. Perhaps my life has been lived out according to parables of losing and finding, embodying the lost coin, the lost sheep and the lost son.

There have been times when my life has been difficult, but never more than I could bear. God is there ready for us to grab when we are on the point of falling, like a lifeline erected on boats in rough weather. I only understood this in retrospect.

I have learned a great deal from living with a prayerful and friendly monastic community. In addition, the Scriptures and the *Rule of Saint Benedict* have helped me to see my whole life in a different perspective. I learned that the Prologue to the *Rule* begins with an almost hidden reference to the Parable of the Prodigal Son. By 'the labour of obedience' the one addressed by the loving Master was to return to him from whom he had strayed by the 'sloth of disobedience'. This certainly resonated with me.

Montefiore found the essence of the Christian Gospel in Lk. 15.1-10, the parables of God's mercy. He wrote:

> Jesus sought to bring back into glad communion with God those whom sin, whether 'moral or ceremonial', had driven away ... He did not avoid sinners, he sought them out. They were still children of God. This was a new and sublime contribution to the development of religion and morality.
>
> (W. Barclay, *Daily Readings* (1991))

This is something which is very important to me as it turns my previous understanding of God upon its head.

When a newcomer enters the monastery, the novice mistress has to test the postulant to see whether she is truly seeking God (*RB* 58). In the Parable of the Prodigal Son, when he has returned to his senses, it is the son who seeks the father. This is what I now have to do, and endeavour to do so in prayer and in the small details of daily life. People sometimes wonder how I could possibly leave my children and grandchildren. The renunciation asked of us in the Gospel seems too harsh – to leave all that we love behind. Yet, in a strange way, I am closer to my family now; as our personal relationship with God deepens it contains our earthly relationships and strengthens them. What we give to God is returned a hundredfold. From this realization I became aware of a paradox: there is no one right way to view God. He can be viewed from every angle, some of them seemingly inconsistent, but every facet reveals an aspect of his nature. This ongoing revelation shows that God can be found everywhere, at any moment.

My understanding of the Psalms has developed: they have so much more meaning than I ever dreamed. Every time we pray, a small detail or insight comes to the fore, or comes to mind while I work in silence. The Psalms express the needs of both all humanity and creation, and thus the Spirit prays within us (cf. Rom. 8.26).This communal prayer is of great importance, and can be psychologically as well as spiritually cleansing.

I am finally beginning to understand what John the Baptist meant when he said: 'He must increase, but I must decrease' (Jn 3.30). Now that I am coming to recognize the greatness of God, I am also beginning to know my own insignificance. This frees me from having to know all the answers, and solving all the problems. I had, all my life, tried to be the one in charge, the competent woman able to face all difficulties. I have come to see my life as though it were the entire field in the Parable of the Sower. God has lavishly scattered the seeds but many have fallen on unprofitable soil. It has taken the constant care and attention of the Farmer to nurture the remaining seed. This he is doing through the Holy Spirit. It is all hidden work.

That day of the Transfiguration in 2002 found me prepared to give myself totally to God within this community of nuns. My children, grandchildren and great-granddaughter, having had five years to adjust to the situation, were there and by their presence and prayers assisted at this oblation, supporting me all the way. We continue to seek God, learning together and from each other. Fresh insights are constantly being given to us. Writing this chapter has freed me, has shown me my need to let go more, to trust God more, to hand over to him the consequences of my sins and mistakes, and the hurts these have caused. The words of St Paul have become my own, 'In everything God works for good with those who love him, who are called according to his purpose' (Rom. 8.28).

Now I know
that all I have lived
has spoken to me of You,
Lord, all that I live now
I live with You.

(Vitorchiano Trappistines)

10

An Away Match

Andrew Nugent

WHAT'S IN A NAME?

My father was born in 1910 and christened Peter Owen. The initials PO proved an embarrassment to him at school, as they designated, colloquially, the chamber-pot, still a familiar utensil in most households 90 years ago. To save me similar raillery, I was launched, 27 years later, with my father's first name only, Peter. I sometimes resented this well-intentioned parsimony. It seemed to signify an insufficient enthusiasm about my arrival for anyone to spend much time thinking up a second name. Besides, even the short name that I did get was already fully occupied by my father, who did not improve matters by sometimes referring to me, wittily, as 'Repeater'.

My name afforded me slight purchase on a tenuous existence. In the Bible, God sometimes changes the names that parents have affixed to their children. I had few regrets about exchanging my own name for Andrew when I became a monk. This was not for any pious reason, but simply because it was a sort of breakthrough, a more emphatic arrival on the planet – like at last getting your own bed or bicycle. At confirmation, my Aunt Kathleen persuaded me to add Bernard to my time-sharing first name. My birthday falls on that saint's feast-day and Aunt Kathleen probably hoped that I might become a Cistercian. I didn't quite make it. She can hardly have known that there was already, so to speak, Cistercian blood in the family. I discovered this myself, 60 years later in Nigeria, when I came across a book called *A Time to Keep Silence* by Patrick Leigh Fermor in the library at St Benedict's Priory where I was novice master at the time. Here is what the book says:

> The founder of [La Grande Trappe] was a Count Rotrou III of Perche, Seigneur of Nogent-le-Rotrou, progenitor of the Nugent family of Ireland, a famous Crusader who fought the Moors in Spain and assisted at the capture of Jerusalem ... The foundation was intended partly as a thank-offering for the Count's safe passage across the English Channel, [and] partly as a memorial to his wife, Princess Matilda, daughter of Henry I of England, who had perished in the loss of the White Ship. This disaster had made so deep an impression on him that he ordered the church to be built in the shape of a reversed sailing vessel, with masts for supporting pillars and an upturned keel as roof-tree, a shape that it retained until the French Revolution.[1]

That history may be a little romanticized, notwithstanding which my monastic vocation may still be described as vaguely 'genetic'. Some people say that all vocations are born, not made. I believe this myself, in the sense that I believe in the slow-release miracle of God's love. From the womb he calls each one of us – perhaps even from all eternity. In my own case, how appropriate, and how coincidental, that I have lived for most of my life in an

211

abbey-castle which displays Henry II and his wife Eleanor of Aquitaine in effigy on its portals. It was on behalf of this Henry that my distinguished ancestor, Gilbert de Nogent, decamped to Ireland in 1172, after that country had been granted to the English crown by Pope Adrian IV, who just happened to be an Englishman himself. Once again, how coincidental and, this time, how *in*appropriate!

TOO SHORT A CHILDHOOD

Kilteevan was a five-bedroom, two-reception-room house with modest gardens fore and aft behind high walls. It was situated at Grey Gates in the South Dublin suburb of Mount Merrion, which in those days was practically out in the countryside. We walked through meadows to Mass in our tiny parish church. I remember every step and turn in the stairway of that house, every article of furniture in it, every flower and shrub in the garden. The smell of lavender will always evoke for me one square foot of magic earth. This was my home, my enchanted castle, my lost domain.

How serene and beautiful seem the reveries of early childhood. I could lose myself for hours in the contemplation of almost anything in that paradise: flowers in a vase, the pattern on a dinner plate, passing clouds seen through a filigree of silver leaves, or, as evening drew in, an open fire where whole worlds came and went before my impassive eye. My mind, Buddha-like, still, perceiving, without need for analysis or discourse, harmonies, things that are, things that could be, mysteries. Gaston Bachelard's expression is so accurate: '*sérieux comme un enfant qui rêve*'.[2]

The springs of childhood memory and imagination are all too soon polluted. Early one comes to know oneself as strangely alienated, exiled, indigent and homeless. The clear pool of one's inner life too soon begins to seethe and bubble with

212

incoherent fears and fantasies, with anger, envy, lust, self-pity and sadness. All spiritualities – and so many quick-fix therapies besides – seek to moderate this witch's cauldron in the soul, to dissipate its noxious vapours. But perhaps, like Socrates, it is only in the moment of death that we can sacrifice that cock in thanksgiving, to Asclepius, the god of healing.

One day, as I was standing alone at the side-gate from our garden onto the public road, a ragged youngster, one of three walking past, with a deft curtain-opening gesture at the seat of his pants, exposed his marble-white backside to my startled gaze. 'Did ya ever see that in your life before?' he asked me tauntingly. More than half a century later, I remember his exact words and intonation. It was probably the first time that anybody outside the family had ever addressed me directly, on my own, and in such a personal way. I was 5 or 6 at the time but this was, unmistakably, an erotic experience – *tremendum et fascinosum* – at once terrifying and thrilling. It was not just the spectacle – I had surely seen bottoms before in my short life. It was the direct interpellation by another human person, and in so intimate a way, that so deeply disconcerted me.

I am 6 or 7. I see a dead man at a bus stop. He is lying geometrically parallel to the edge of the footpath, his head to the bus stop, his feet neatly aligned. He is covered by a blanket but I know that he is dressed in a brown suit. There seems to be nobody else around, just me and the corpse, waiting for its bus. I am horrified by its total immobility. The pavement and the bus stop are still but they, at least, are sleeping partners in a consortium of movement. The corpse is a parasite on the universe, in the world but not of it, sucking at the slender nexus of my being. I don't think these things: I know them. I tell nobody.

Sex and Death: Somebody or something is preparing me for life, making best use of local talent.

MY MOTHER

She was 36 and I, the second of her four sons, was 8. I remember her vividly, but little of what she did or said. I feel her gentle total presence with me, her kisses, her caress. I hear her soft singing, the mild prayers she taught me. I recall once, standing on a chair while she was drying me after a bath. I am begging her to teach me *another* prayer. She had to think. Eventually, she came up with the *Hail, Holy Queen.*

She had been in bed for days, wretchedly sick. Downstairs the house seemed cold and empty. Coming in from altar-serving in Mount Merrion church on Sunday (Benediction – I had not yet graduated to Mass), I was conscious, for the first time in my life, of feeling lonely and depressed. They said she had gastric flu. By the time the surgeon was called, her stomach had swollen like a pregnant woman's: her appendix had burst. In those days before antibiotics, there was little hope. She died in the Mater Hospital on 28 September, 1945.

Next morning, I remember Dad giving us porridge in the kitchen. He was unshaven, red-eyed and ugly. I hated how he scraped the burnt porridge off the bottom of the saucepan. Even in the next millennium, the very sight or smell of porridge fills me with revulsion. Dad said, 'It is too nice a day to go to school.' We pretended to believe this meaningless excuse for being confined to our bedroom all morning. It was exactly like when we were being punished. Later we were taken to our paternal grandmother's house. She sat at the head of the table in the basement dining-room, holding my father's hand. My brother and I sat opposite him eating lunch. 'Do you know what Mammy has done to us?' Dad asked with painful lightness, 'she has gone off to heaven'. I immediately resented this mock-comic blaming of my mother. I inquired acidly, 'Do you mean she is dead?' Half-a-century later, I learned that the adults present on the occasion were impressed and appalled. Of feelings I remember nothing except an enormous black paralysis.

It is 60 years since I left my childhood home forever. I have never gone back there, even when I could have. Why not? I think, because I knew in my heart – if not in my head – that the rest of my life was going to be an away match. In retrospect, I think that this was when I embarked on my monastic journey, this strange *peregrinatio*.

When, soon after, Dad came to visit us in boarding-school he made to kiss me on the mouth as we had always done. I twisted my face sideways so that his lips landed awkwardly on my ear. Laughing but uneasy, he exclaimed, 'What are you doing? You kiss like a nun.'

O clever prophetic man!

SCHOOL

Apart from infants' school with the Dominican Nuns at Sion Hill, my entire primary and secondary education, from 1945 to 1955, was entrusted to the Holy Ghost Fathers, first at Willow Park, then at Blackrock College. For the first eight years I was a boarder. This was just after the Second World War. Food was scarce. There was porridge, of course: I could not eat it – even to save my life. My most indelible memory of school is of cold and hunger. In a desperate attempt to supplement the meagre diet, the school authorities decreed mandatory dosing with cod-liver oil. That could have made some difference, but we routinely queued up to receive our regulation mouthful, then ran to the urinals and spat it out. Not surprisingly, I was undersized and suffered from a host of minor ailments:

chilblains, boils, head-lice, dandruff, rotten teeth, and, in due course, horrific acne.

Personality-wise, I was not an attractive little boy. Perhaps nobody can reach a child who has lost his mother. Thick layers of frozen ice protect this bleeding heart from the wound of love and from the risk of further betrayal. I became out-of-reach, impenetrable, old-mannish – my first headmaster, in exasperation, christened me 'grandfather' – at the age of 8. I was full of myself, a mocker, often insolent, not a natural child. Not daring to let my own defences down, I envied other boys with all my heart, those whose spontaneous words and actions reflected their limpid souls. In me there was little spontaneity and no limpidity. I manufactured my reactions and responses, then squinted out from my bunker to see what effect they were having. In the process I acquired many skills and proficiencies: wit, dialectic, a cruel instinct for other people's weak points, and a talent for lying. Over the years I hope that my more immoral arts have been lost, and the rest humanized, even baptized. But at that time, I was not a nice boy, and I knew it. Plus I was zero at games and a mediocre student.

Orphans or 'near-orphans' play an important part in the novels I write: David, in *The Four Courts Murder*; Pita, in *Second Burial*; and Seán and Eddie, in *Soul Murder* (to appear). Actually, it was only when I came to write this chapter that I realized what I have been doing. All these waifs are, in fact, myself – boys dealt a tough hand, and coping with it courageously – as I would love to have coped with the hand that I was dealt, but didn't.

When I began to have girlfriends I could not shake off the idea that there must be some terrible mistake. The competition was awesome. An army of hunks, jocks, tennis aces, dancers of the fandango, and post-graduate Casanovas was marshalled in serried ranks against me. So why

216

me? Eventually I concluded that some girls just have bad taste.

UNIVERSITY

I studied Law at King's Inns and a range of arts subjects at University College Dublin. The subjects fascinated me, particularly history and psychology, and several forensic disciplines. When examination results began to come in, I was pleased to learn that I was quite bright – something that had simply not occurred to me before I was 18. I had begun debating in my senior years in Blackrock and thoroughly enjoyed it. I continued at college, in the Literary and Historical Society, and at King's Inns. The Inns had the advantage of a good dinner before the debate with a half bottle of Médoc to loosen the tongue. Quite unexpectedly, it was in the context of a debate that I was made to think again about what I was doing with my life. This was a gala debate to mark the centenary of the Literary and Historical Society. A team of students was to debate against a team of the great and the good of former years. I was privileged to be among the bright-eyed young orators. Whether or not Médoc played any part, the speech was a success. At the reception afterwards Professor Robin Dudley-Edwards, who had taught me, and my mother before me, told me that some terribly famous person sitting beside him had said when I had finished speaking: 'Isn't it a terrible shame to think of that delightful fellow ending up as a dry-as-dust old lawyer?'

I know many lawyers who have not ended up 'dry-as-dust old lawyers'. But how would it be for *me*? That was the question; and it would not go away.

THE BAR

I was called to the bar in October 1959 and plied my trade for two years in Dublin and on the Midland Circuit. My father was a Senior Counsel; my brother and several relatives were solicitors. This meant that I had a leg up and was quickly, if modestly, gainfully employed. In military terms, I saw action. When I was leaving school in 1955 I had seriously considered a religious or priestly vocation. I would then have joined the missionary congregation of my teachers at Blackrock, many of whom had made a deep impression on me. A worldly-wise uncle gave me some advice which he said had been given him in turn by a saintly priest. 'Don't be a priest – unless you cannot possibly help it.' I thought that this was splendid advice. After all, I reasoned, God is big enough to get what he wants. So like Jonah the Prophet, I decided to give him a run for his money.

Actually, I think that the Lord, too, thought that it was excellent advice. From the age of 8 I had been institutio-nalized in all-male environments. I didn't even have a sister. I really needed to get out and see the world – and especially girls. For six years of university and as a young barrister, I had a ball. And for those six years of sheer enjoyment and real achievement, I felt that God was very close to me. I prayed often and never consciously displeased him. I cannot say that of any other period in my life, before or since. I was not half grateful enough to God for making it possible, and even easy to love him. It was as if the Spirit was saying to me: 'Do not be afraid. Spread your wings!'

But all those years I had really been reserving judgement. It was time to decide. In my second year at the bar I had doubled my earnings. My practice was building up rapidly. Soon it would take me over. Is that what I really wanted?

Did I really intend to spend 30 or 40 years aiming to be a High Court Judge, Chief Justice, Attorney General, or whatever? The answer was, frankly, no. Next question, was I going to get married? I knew some lovely girls with whom I could have been very happy. And yet, somehow, I knew in my heart that heaven – for whatever reason – had simply neglected to make a match for me.

It took me at least 30 years more to grow into the mystery of celibacy. The Spirit is working in the life of each one of us, but it is slow work: we are *the slow-release miracle* of God's love.³ In my middle 20s, in relation to celibacy, I was at least clear about what I was being asked to undertake or to forego. It is my belief that nobody should embark on or continue in monastic life without this basic realization and firm commitment. Any equivocation on this point can lead later to the most sordid of compromises and even – as we sadly know – to the gravest of crimes.

GLENSTAL

Why a monastery? And why Glenstal? The choice surprised even myself. I knew Glenstal because my two younger brothers had gone to school there. Also, three years running, I had done the Holy Week Retreat at Glenstal with a group of friends from Blackrock College. Even in the pre-Vatican II era, this had been a fascinating discovery of what liturgy was about. The simplicity of the monks' lives also appealed to me. The first time I saw a monastic cell, I said instinctively: 'This is for me.' Perhaps ten foot square, bare boards for a floor, it was furnished with an iron bedstead, table and chair, a prie-dieu, a washstand with bucket and basin, two shelves for books, three for clothes, and a crucifix for only ornament. Even still, I hate clutter. In that respect at least, I travel light.

But I could have had liturgy and simplicity elsewhere, and I would have preferred an Order where they did parish work, went to the cinema, smoked cigarettes, and had an occasional gin and tonic. But God wanted something else of me. I have always had the strong feeling that the choice was his and that he hijacked me into Glenstal without, initially anyhow, giving me much of a clue about what I was letting myself in for. I took it on trust – and there were plenty of shocks, and rude awakenings to come, and some thin times during the next 46 years. Nevertheless, I have been given the precious gift never once to doubt my vocation. *Suscipe me, Domine, et vivam!* That is what we cry out on the day of our Profession. If the Lord upholds me – I shall *live*. He *does* uphold me, and I *do* live.

The first three years were difficult. I had only the vaguest notions about monastic spirituality when I entered Glenstal. It soon seemed to me that I had embarked on some ghastly trip in a time machine back to the Dark Ages. The monastic restoration of the late nineteenth century had been a highly romantic, not to say reactionary enterprise. Whatever the monks of the Ages of Faith did, we did too, enthusiastically. It was like a game of 'Let's play being monks' – and I should have been much more playful. We had Chapters of Faults and practised exotic penances. The more observant brethren even had their own peculiar way of talking, for instance, describing everything as 'ours', just stopping short of 'our handkerchief' and 'our toothbrush'.

One could smile at all this – and it was not really important. But the coexistence in this way of life of so much that was genuinely sublime and the few things that were truly ridiculous produced in me an enormous tension. Who was I to say what was sublime and what ridiculous? So I forced myself to do everything with the same horrified dedication. Above all, the spirituality seemed to my untutored mind so negative. I wanted to be generous, to love God and everyone else. Instead of which we seemed to be fed a diet of guilt and 'compunction' – whatever that might be. We spent a lot of our time in the 'sin bin' 'making satisfaction' for involuntary fouls, while reciting the *Miserere*, the monks' favourite psalm, which we had at least twice every day. It was full of great lines like,

> 'O see, in guilt I was born,
> a sinner was I conceived'.
>
> (Ps. 50[51].7)

So much for my poor mother!

Besides, this dismal perspective began to become a self-fulfilling prophecy. From a man of integrity who could stand up straight and look God in the eye, I seemed to be deteriorating into something despicable, increasingly infested with the most shameful and humiliating demons: envy, pride, anger, gluttony, sadness and, of course, our all-weather companion, lust. In my monastic journey I seemed to be going at speed in precisely the wrong direction. I could only hold on desperately to a single thought: that God, for some crazy reason, wanted me to continue with a race where I was knocking all the hurdles. I trusted him. Fortunately, I had many kind and wise confrères, my seniors and betters in the monastic life, and especially, I had an admirable novice master, our future Abbot Augustine O'Sullivan. He did not rush in with erudite discourses about the *logismoi* – the eight demons of monastic tradition. He knew that I had to go through it, so he just held me by the hand, metaphorically. I count it a privilege that, as he lay dying in Africa 40 years later, I was there to hold his hand, literally, to the end.

Most of the things in my early monastic formation that I

221

found perplexing or repugnant were to do with externals. They have been modified or discarded long since. In the more serious issues of spirituality, it is true that there was a residue of Jansenism in the Irish Church well into the 1960s and 1970s. This, combined with traditional monastic spirituality, could make a pretty toxic mix. If I had been a less uptight person, and also less sure of my judgements of people and situations, I might have had an easier ride.

More generally and very happily, there has been an extraordinary flowering of monastic studies over the last half-century that has made it easier for people like me to appreciate the rich treasures we possess in the monastic tradition and, most especially, in the *Rule of St Benedict*. I am glad too – at least in retrospect – that my vocation was properly tested, in the sense that I was forced to confront myself, to know my fragility, and to dig deeper. It seems to me that if people in formation are not afforded these opportunities – and, specifically, the chance to confront self-will, which the universal tradition recognizes as the core problem for monastics – there is a real danger that their vocations will never mature and a high probability that they will be in serious trouble later in life. Unfortunately, I have seen this happen.

STRASBOURG AND VATICAN II

I was sent to Strasbourg University to study Theology and was there from 1964 to 1968, four golden years. This was the era of Vatican II, a most exciting time to be studying theology. The giants among our professors were Chavasse, Schmitt, Nédoncelle, and Vogel. Several of the others did not survive – as teachers – the Student Revolution of 1968. I was living in a *Séminaire International* run by the French Oratorians, just across a pleasant park from the Council of

Europe, and scarcely ten minutes walk from the *Palais Universitaire*. We were a happy community of 14 or 15 nationalities, the majority being French.

During holidays I travelled widely, hitch-hiking everywhere. It was a great way to see Europe, and also to learn French. Where else could you get a person to sit and talk to you hour after hour? Even more importantly, I had stumbled into a real pastoral need and a genuine apostolate. To my amazement, in 90 per cent of the cars, as soon as the driver realized that I was a monk, he wanted to talk about his soul. Most of these people had not darkened the door of a church in decades. Some of them did not believe in God. But their spiritual hunger was voracious. So often, even the non-believers would say when I was leaving – and sometimes reeling out of – their cars, 'Brother, pray for me!'

This was only 20 years after the Second World War. We were in the heart of Europe. I was not yet a priest, but I heard many heartbreaking stories, things that people had kept bottled up within themselves for years – things too tragic, or too evil to tell. Then, one day, a wayfarer appears, one with some claim to represent God's pity, one who is non-threatening, who has to beg for a lift, and one whom they will never see again. Several times in these circumstances, the floodgates opened. Some of what people told me was very difficult to listen to. Once or twice I was literally physically afraid of what I was hearing. And, yes, I *did* learn French, some of it not contained in any respectable phrasebook.

From the monastic point of view, I was the archetypical gyrovague of Benedict's *Rule* (Chapter 1), spending time in so many monasteries and being welcomed with Benedictine and Cistercian hospitality everywhere. Those years of the Vatican Council were so exhilarating and so hopeful for the universal Church, but also for the *ecclesiolae*, the micro-churches, of our different communities. Because I was studying theology outside a monastic milieu, I particularly valued opportunities to sit at the feet of scholars and sages in our monasteries – and also of many superiors who, I suspect, found in me, and in other birds of passage, more seemingly docile minds than they were accustomed to find amongst their own foot soldiers. These were wise and experienced men who taught me many interesting things about monastic life. Then there were the foot soldiers themselves. How many dreams we dreamed, how many visions we saw, about what was to happen in our monasteries, in the Church, and in the whole wide world!

THE SCHOOL

I was ordained in 1968 on the feast of St Louis of France – a nice touch which I appreciated in view of my origins and formation. Under the influence of the *moine-non-prêtre* movement I had hesitated for a year in order to be sure that I had a priestly vocation. In the end, I decided that this was what I had always wanted. Conscious of my unworthiness, I went ahead. I was 31 years of age.

For the next quarter-century, with the exception of two years in Africa, I was immersed in the life of the school. Even periods as bursar – when I had no money –and as novice master – when I had no novices – did not interrupt this involvement. I was teaching French and Religion, occasionally English and, for most of the time, I was either Housemaster for Seniors or Headmaster. Initially, I found close contact with teenage boys alarming. Could I control them? And, a much more fundamental question, could I control myself? To be frank, I found the closeness, physical and emotional, to boys – in dormitories and showers, in changing rooms and, above all, in the inner spaces of my

224

own psyche and theirs – threatening. Besides, as every experienced housemaster learns, there is a possibility, perhaps even a likelihood, that some boys, uncertain about their own sexuality, may attempt confusedly to lead an adult into an emotional, and even a physical relationship. That happens, and when it does, the onus is 100 per cent on the adult's side to act with total integrity.

Accordingly, I started off pretty gruff, to maintain a safe distance between the boys and myself. When I learned to have more confidence in God's love, manifested in my own charisma, I became more able to help boys to negotiate difficult passages in their own lives. They trusted me and I did not betray that trust. I am so grateful to God for this grace – and humbly proud of it – if that is not too much of a paradox. In one of my novels I have tried to express what my feelings are when I look back on this phase of my life:

'I pray for those boys, all of them, every day of my life.'
Quilligan was touched. As they walked to his car, he said, 'Can you really love *all* of them?'
The old priest replied sadly, 'Nowadays, a priest could hardly dare admit to loving *any* of them. I am not sure anyhow if love is the right word. I *pity* all of them. Life can be lonely and cruel, and each of them has so little to throw into the struggle, just that little bundle of bones, gas, and guts, and a few bits of brains, for whatever that's worth. I think compassion is all that we can do. That is love, in a way, isn't it?'[4]

The word compassion comes from *cum patior* meaning to *suffer with*. So Christ is described in the Letter to the Hebrews as 'a compassionate high priest'. I did not really have much of a childhood myself. I think now that part of the meaning of what happened was to make me able to understand and sympathize with what other children were to go through.

THE FRENCH TRIP

And then there was the French Trip, which in the dying years of the second millennium, was probably the only surviving *rite de passage* in the northern hemisphere. As good as anything going on up the Amazon Valley or down in equatorial rain forests, it was Europe's nearest equivalent to circumcision with a blunt-edged flint. Ostensibly, this was an annual cycling/camping expedition of two weeks duration to Normandy, Brittany, or the Loire Valley. I led 18 of those sorties between 1970 and 1993.

Once at Rosslare, where we were taking the ferry, a mother said to me, 'Father, you don't know how lucky you are.' Faced at that moment with having to feed 38 persons three times a day for the next two weeks, I was not feeling particularly lucky. 'They are only 15,' she added, 'but they won't come on holidays with us any more.'

For many people, nomadic camping is a way of life, not a game; indeed it is a powerful metaphor for life itself. My personal discovery was that, having envisaged an entertainment, I had found a spirituality, one which affected me profoundly, as I know it affected and changed many, perhaps even most of those who travelled with me.

Three times in Glenstal we have had the sadness of a boy dying while still at school. Is it just a macabre coincidence that each of these three boys had, in his own turn, embarked on the French Trip within a year or less of his own death? Is it foolish to suggest that, in each boy's case, this experience had taught him something that helped prepare him for that longest journey of all? I have personal reasons to believe that this is so.

226

'Spirituality', of course, is a big word, so let me concede that I am talking about a *small*, unpretentious spirituality, accessible to youngsters and simple people – and definitely not for spiritual gourmets or snobs. This spirituality has two aspects, the *tent*, and the *journey*.

THE TENT

We are talking about real camping, of course, not that ridiculous charade of collapsible grand pianos and inflatable everything else. So let me say three things that I have learnt about living in a tent – or indeed in a monastery, because St Benedict uses the word 'tent' (*tabernaculum*) four times in the Prologue of his *Rule* to describe living in a monastery.

A tent is a place of humility. You sleep on the *humus*, the good earth, from which we come, and to which we shall one day return.

A tent is a place of sharing, where there is no pretence or privacy, not even air space or personal oxygen.

A tent is a place where I am one with Creation. It is a living membrane, stirring with the wind, pulsating with the earth, trembling, fragile and beautiful. In the deep silence of the night, our little tent opens upon the measureless beauty of the sea and the stars, of the whole vast universe.

THE JOURNEY

A number of things in my life have helped me to understand and to go deeper into the mystery of celibacy as a personal vocation. Firstly, the bitterness of losing my mother at so early an age and leaving my childhood home forever. My life was to be the 'away match' which I have used for the title of this essay – and I could even say for my title deeds, because my inheritance was to be a 'stranger and a nomad

227

on earth'. 'People who speak thus make it clear that they are seeking a [real] homeland' (Heb. 11.14).

Experiences like the weeks I spent hitch-hiking as a student, travelling light, or leading my 'holy people' in our peregrinations through France, though uncomfortable and short on security, have always been resonant for me as to what my *hidden* life, my *real* life, is all about. There is an intriguing paradox in the monastic way of life. We vow *stability* but our life is to be living in tents while we look forward to a city founded, designed, and built by God (cf. Heb. 11.10).

The text of Scripture that has become most significant for me in making sense of celibacy is the one which says that: 'Foxes have holes, and birds of the air have nests; but the Son of man has nowhere to lay his head' (Lk. 9.58). This is saying more than that Jesus has no permanent address. It means that no wife, no children await his return. He has nowhere to lay his head: there is no breast, no shoulder, no lips where he can lay his head, his cheek, his lips.[5] I believe that every person, married or celibate, has this pilgrim dimension to his or her life. Sometimes we are obliged to act out existentially this deep strand in our being. This is the experience of refugees, of immigrants within our own settled and comfortable societies. But it can also be a question of an inner journey where, outwardly, everything seems to be stable and secure but, at the core of our being, we are lost and searching. The *journey* can be voluntarily chosen, too, as do many who undertake the *Camino de Santiago* or some other genuine pilgrimage.

I would envisage our humble cycling trips in this way. They gave youngsters, at a very impressionable age, a glimpse of something very deep in their own make-up. Thirty years later, they have not forgotten. And neither have I.

In Glenstal, for as long as I can remember, we have had a hostel for 'Men of the Road'. Wayfarers, wanderers, these are some of the most marginalized people in society because they wish to be, and indeed probably *need* to live on the very margins of society, like the wandering monks of Russia. Some of these men are probably very close to God. I feel certain that they have won many favours for our community.

AFRICA

My involvement in Africa has been gradual and progressive: a first dipping of the toe into tropical waters for three months in the summer of 1979, followed by two years (1985–87) when I had finished being headmaster. Finally – unless there are surprises still to come – a more serious commitment, as novice master, from 1993 to 2000. All of these stays were spent at St Benedict's Priory, first at Eke in Igboland, subsequently at Ewu-Ishan in Edo State. St Benedict's was a foundation of Glenstal, with initial and significant help from Ampleforth Abbey, notably by the participation of Dom Columba Cary-Elwes. Over the years, 14 monks of Glenstal have sojourned in Ewu. Two of these have left their bones there, victims of malaria, and at least three more have nearly done the same thing as a result of various hazards.

In the space of 30 years St Benedict's has grown to number 30 professed monks, eight of them priests. On 11 July 2006 the monastery acceded to independence and became a conventual priory. The community is thriving. Its works include, as well as a significant pastoral outreach, a large guesthouse, farm, poultry, bakery, shop, and a very impressive herbal clinic. These activities mean that over 80 weekly pay packets arrive into as many local homes. This is a drop in the ocean in a country where there are so many people living on the edge. At the same time, it is not nothing.[6]

During my six years as novice master I had care of 30 novices, 12 of whom have stayed the course and made Final Profession. As well as caring for those who entered the novitiate, I was probably involved in trying to help discern the vocations of well over a hundred young men. Some of these were quite unsuitable for monastic life but, in so far as I can judge, the great majority were sincere and thoroughly likeable. Many were simply looking for an education and for an opportunity to advance themselves in the world. Who could possibly blame them for that?

African young people are very good at telling their stories. Between what I heard in a chaplaincy which I held at Auchi Polytech and in our own novitiate, I must have material for at least a dozen novels. What astonished and never failed to move me was the courage and self-sacrifice with which these youngsters would adhere to the faith or to pursuing a religious vocation. In those earlier years, we had responsibility for several churches and outstations within a wide radius of the monastery. On a typical Sunday morning, I would drive 12 miles to the Polytech at Auchi, a solidly Muslim town with, however, a very dynamic Catholic presence in the student body. I will never forget those young people, their singing and dancing, their drumming, their sheer joy in the faith. If the celebration lasted less than two hours, they would feel positively short-changed. I knew the personal situations of several of these young men and women, the sacrifices they were making for their faith, the temptations besieging them, their sheer goodness and generosity. I owe them far more in terms of edification than they owe to me.

But my Sunday morning was not finished. After Auchi I would head for a large parish church in a town called Jattu. Another two-hour celebration and more fabulous drumming and singing. I would arrive back at the monastery at midday, exhausted, elated, and drenched from head to toe in sweat – no polite euphemism will do justice to the situation 'on the ground'.

How did Nigeria help me on my own monastic journey? I spent nine years in Africa. There I believe that God fashioned for me a soul. First of all because, if the fear of the Lord is the beginning of wisdom – and, as a naturally timorous person, I had a headstart – for those nine years I was more or less scared all the time. Scared of what? Of furious drumming deep in the forest by night, of armed robbers, of diseases, of snakes – I killed eight in my own room – and scorpions, and dogs, and cats, and squirrels and anything else that could have rabies; scared, too, of road accidents. Every single day that I went out onto the road, I saw yet another car, bus or lorry with its wheels in the air. Everyone in Nigeria has his or her own accident eventually. When my time came, in the split second before I lost consciousness, I was vividly aware of someone sitting beside me to protect me. Although somewhat knocked about in the collision, I did survive handsomely. The pragmatic fact is that I had been quite alone in the car on that day. *Nobody* was sitting beside me to protect me. But the greater fact is that I am never alone. I grew to trust in God, simply because there was nobody else – and least of all myself.

Then, too, in Africa, I witnessed people whom I had known to be good slowly becoming great. The Spirit had challenged them to go that extra mile – and they went it. During my last year in Nigeria, within three months of each other, my two companion monks from Ireland both died. They had given everything. They sleep in the good red soil of Africa. But above all, I see my encounter with the people of Nigeria as one of the greatest graces of my entire life.

THE REMAINS OF THE DAY

It was towards the end of my time in Africa that I started writing novels. I had a bad conscience about this, thinking that the descent from reality into fantasy was inappropriate for a monk. I rationalized it as a legitimate form of escapism during a difficult period in my life, when alternative distractions – such as television or the pub – were not available. The profit motive was not an issue, because I never imagined that anyone would publish what I was writing. Moreover, I needed to do this exploration of my inner landscape for myself, first and foremost, before even thinking that it could be useful, instructive, or simply entertaining for other people. It was only slowly that I discovered that what I was trying to do was not to escape but, on the contrary, to be present to myself in a new and deeper way. Whether that took the form of stories, or whether I was writing spirituality or even theology, I wanted to give an account of the things that life has taught me, and especially of the hope that is in me. I think that we – the ten collaborators in this book – have all been engaged in that same project: giving an account of the hope that is in all of us (cf. 1 Pet. 3.15).

Dame Laurentia has asked me, as guest contributor, to add a short conclusion, reflecting briefly on the previous nine monastic journeys. Deeply conscious of the compliment being paid to me, as also of the responsibility that I was assuming, I decided that, like John Cassian in the fourth century, I should visit each of these ammas and abbas in

An Away Match

their respective desert cells. I would sit at their feet and beg
a word from each of them – and so become wise.
  This is what they said:

ABBA MARTIN

'A way of living which tries to put other people first in the
nitty-gritty of daily life: I understood that this was what it
meant to be a Christian. It is in trying to live this Gospel
way of life that we gradually penetrate more and more into
the mysteries of the faith.'

AMMA JOANNA

'I was hungry for life: full of an aching desire for happiness.
The search for happiness will always mean confronting that
paradox Christ presents in the Gospels: if we truly wish to
find fulfilment we must lose our lives by offering life to others
and building our life in God alone.'

AMMA MONICA

'The renunciation asked of us in the Gospel seems too harsh
– to leave all that we love behind. Yet, in a strange way, I
am closer to my family now; as our personal relationship
with God deepens it contains our earthly relationships and
strengthens them. What we give to God is returned a
hundredfold.'

ABBA ALBAN

'What matters is not what I am trying to do for God but
what God does for me in loving me and sustaining me in my
search for him. It has taken me a long time to realize that

self-seeking never leads to discovery of one's true self, for it is only in seeking God that we find ourselves.'

AMMA AGNES

'There are several fundamentals common to all Benedictines, such as liturgy, personal prayer, asceticism, *lectio divina*, study, community life, manual labour, but within that framework the journey of each one is unique.'

AMMA LAURENTIA

'"A melody beyond me, yet intimately myself": this theme tune has run right through my monastic life to date and I suspect will run and run, for it is the tune of our Benedictine vows of obedience, *conversatio* and stability, vows which are rooted in Christ's own obedience to the Father.'

ABBA MICHAEL

'Someone asked a monk, "What do you do in the monastery?" The monk replied, "We fall and get up, we fall and get up." This is my only expectation in monastic life: to continue my journey toward God with the help of my brothers, falling and getting up again, helping them as well.'

ABBA SIMON

'Just to think back over the human opportunities, the enjoyment and the freedom makes me realize how uniquely blessed I have been by God. I do not think I would ever have been so happy in another walk of life. For all this I have done nothing. I have merely been the son who said "No", initially. I sometimes wonder whether, had I said

"Yes", and also been willing to go, God would have called me in the first place.'

ABBA DAVID

'Perhaps the lesson that I have gradually learnt is the importance of patience, of knowing that often the only thing we can do is put ourselves and others in the way of grace and create a kind of hopeful space where people can let God work.'

I knew an old monk once in a monastery far away who had been sent to a foundation of his European abbey in the pious hope that he would find something useful to do, something he was good at, something to afford him a little sense of fulfilment and achievement in life. He had not found any of this in his monastery of origin and, in the event, he was not to find it in his new monastic home either. The fact is that he was not really good at anything and during a great number of years – because he lived to be a very old man – he was, in human terms, comprehensively useless and achieved nothing. His saving grace, from the community's point of view, was that he was no trouble: his needs were few, he was not demanding, and he did not get in the way of those dynamic confrères who tend to abound in young foundations.

I came upon this old man one day sitting in the monastery garden. This was just months before he died. 'What do you do all day now, Father?' I asked, not maliciously I hope – because the factual answer to my question would surely have had to be, 'nothing'. I asked simply for the sake of saying something. He gave me a beautiful smile and said, 'Oh, that is easy! I thank God; I just thank God all day.' I did not ask incredulously, 'For what?' because I realized at once in my heart that if only I could end my own days thanking God ceaselessly, my life would have been enormously worthwhile. Indeed, if I end my life any other way, what will it all have been about?[7]

NOTES

1. P. Leigh Fermor (1957), *A Time to Keep Silence*. London: John Murray, pp. 56–7.
2. English has no equivalent of *rêve* in the sense that Bachelard uses the word. 'Dream' is too much and 'day-dream' is too little. That is why we use the French word 'reverie'.
3. I have tried to develop these ideas – and indeed whatever few thoughts I may have about the spiritual life – in *The Slow-Release Miracle* (2006). Dublin: Columba Press/Mahwah NJ: Paulist Press.
4. *The Four Courts Murder* (2006). Dublin: Headline, p. 173.
5. See my article, 'One man's celibacy', *The Tablet* (14 January, 1995), substantially reproduced in *The Slow-Release Miracle*.
6. *The Benedictine Yearbook 2007* (published by EBC Trading Ltd) contains two informative articles about this monastery.
7. This story appears in *The Slow-Release Miracle*.

Epilogue

Waiting

waiting in autumn
for new leaves
the dying summer
not forgotten

waiting in winter
closed to the world
as snow leaves white
was still is rotten

waiting in hope
of calmer seas
and persons with whom
to share laughter

waiting in trust
against all pain
that God's hand
will dissolve disaster

waiting for spring
and new love
the child's wisdom
finds nothing fright'ning

waiting in dark
storm blinded
for the Father's shaft
of eternal lightning

©Ralph Wright OSB
St Louis Abbey